Contents

Summary

Each year, on average, almost 250 million people are affected by 'natural' disasters.[1] In a typical year between 1998 and 2007, 98 per cent of them suffered from climate-related disasters such as droughts and floods rather than, for example, devastating but relatively rare events such as earthquakes. According to new research for this report, by 2015 this could grow by more than 50 per cent to an average of over 375 million affected by climate-related disasters each year.[2]

Any such projection is not an exact science, but it is clear that substantially more people may be affected by disasters in the very near, not just distant, future, as climate change and environmental mismanagement create a proliferation of droughts, landslides, floods and other local disasters. And more people will be vulnerable to them because of their poverty and location.[3]

Some of these environmental changes will also increase the threat of new conflicts, which will mean more people displaced, and more need for humanitarian aid. One recent report estimated that 46 countries will face a 'high risk of violent conflict' when climate change exacerbates traditional security threats.[4] Already, there is evidence that the number of conflicts is again on the rise,[5] while the threat of long-running conflicts creating vast new humanitarian demands was painfully shown by the upsurge of violence in the eastern Democratic Republic of Congo in 2008.

In short, by 2015, an unprecedented level of need for humanitarian assistance could overwhelm the world's current humanitarian capacity.

Already, many governments fail to cope with threats like storms, floods and earthquakes. They fail to act quickly or effectively enough in response to these events, or to take preventative action to reduce unnecessary deaths and suffering. Indeed, the very actions of some governments and their national elites place marginalised people at risk from disasters by discriminating against them, like those forced to live in flimsy slum housing so easily destroyed by floods and landslips.

At the same time, international humanitarian assistance is often too slow or inappropriate, and the UN-led reforms since 2005 to improve it have only begun to make a difference.

Challenge

The scale of the humanitarian challenge is unprecedented. National and donor governments, aid agencies, and others must act to improve the quality and quantity of humanitarian aid. Whether or not there is the political will to do this will be one of the defining features of our age, and will dictate whether millions live or die.

Even in daunting economic times, the world can afford to meet the humanitarian needs of every person struggling to survive a disaster. It is possible to reduce the threats from climate-related catastrophes. It is possible for governments to provide good-quality aid to their citizens.

And it will cost a tiny fraction of what rich countries spent on the global financial crisis since 2008 to provide decent humanitarian assistance to all those men, women, and children who, by 2015, may need it. If all Organisation for Economic Co-operation and Development (OECD) governments simply gave as much (per head of their population) as the OECD's ten most generous countries did in 2006, global humanitarian aid would increase to a total of $42bn.[6] In 2008, European governments found $2.3 trillion to provide guarantees for their financial sectors: the German and UK governments alone found $68bn and $40bn to bail out just two banks, Hypo Real Estate and the Royal Bank of Scotland.[7] Decent aid, for every person in need, would be a bargain by comparison.

Rich governments must also take the lead in mitigating the impact of climate change, a key factor in driving the increased threat of disaster. In accordance with their responsibility (for greenhouse gas emissions) and capability (to mobilise resources), rich countries must cut global emissions so that global warming stays as far below 2°C as possible, and provide at least $50bn per year to help poor countries adapt to already unavoidable climate change.

But the governments of developing countries must also take greater responsibility for responding to disasters and reducing people's vulnerability to them. The growth in localised climate-related shocks will hit people in developing countries hardest, because their homes and livelihoods will be most vulnerable. So developing countries will need to enable regional authorities and civil society to respond effectively.

More vulnerable people

For millions of women and men worldwide it is their vulnerability – who they are, where they live, and how they make a living – and not the threats they face per se that will determine whether they survive. Vulnerability to threats such as conflict or environmental hazards like floods and earthquakes is a direct result of poverty; the political choices, corruption, and greed that cause it, and the political indifference that allows it to endure.

In 2008, in the devastated Haitian city of Gonaïves, Ogè Léandre, a 45-year-old father of six, had a lucky escape:

> The water started to rise, and it did not stop ... the water was already so high and strong that I could not hold on to one of my children and the water swept her away. Luckily someone was there to grab her. We got to the roof-top of the [hurricane] shelter, and, about an hour later, watched as our entire house was washed away.[8]

The tropical storms of 2008 wreaked havoc in Haiti. In Gonaïves alone, up to a quarter of the population were forced from their homes, as tens of thousands of poorly constructed and badly sited slum houses were swept away.[9] Everywhere, poor people are the most vulnerable to being killed or made destitute by disasters. In rich countries, an average of 23 people die in any given disaster; in the least-developed countries this is 1,052.[10] This is because poor people like Ogè and his children often live in poorly constructed homes on land threatened by flooding, drought and landslips, and in areas without effective health services or infrastructure. Some groups – women and girls, the chronically sick, the elderly, and others – are even more vulnerable, their ability to cope limited by discrimination, inequality, or their physical health. In both conflict and natural disaster, women's and girls' vulnerability to sexual violence and abuse increases as communities and families are broken up, and local authorities lose control of law and order.

But for families living in poverty, the cumulative effect of more frequent disasters will drive them into a vicious cycle of vulnerability to further shocks. The poorer one is, the less resilient one's livelihood, the fewer assets one has to sell to survive a crisis, and the longer it takes to recover. A 2004 study of the impact of instances of low rainfall on subsistence farmers in Ethiopia found that it often took households years to recover from such shocks.[11]

4

Looking to the future, the point is this: for many of the world's poor people, vulnerability to disaster may increase, and there are four trends that may drive this. First, there are far more people living in urban slums built on precarious land. Second, the increasing pressure on rural productive land, caused by drought, population density, and increasing demand for meat and dairy products in emerging economies, means that more people will find it difficult to get enough to eat. Third, climate change, environmental degradation and conflict may drive more people from their homes, stripping them of their livelihoods, assets, and their networks of family and communities that can support them. Some estimates suggest that up to one billion people will be forced to move from their homes by 2050.[12] Finally, the global economic crisis that escalated in late 2008 may increase unemployment and undermine social safety nets which, in some countries, may contribute to increased humanitarian needs.

Choosing to act

There are positive trends as well, and they can be built on. Not everyone has become more vulnerable to the rising number of disasters. In some countries, the proportion of people living in poverty has fallen, allowing more people to have secure homes and livelihoods, and to build up savings that help them recover from shocks.[13] Other countries have a proven record of saving lives. In many countries, the death toll from disasters has been drastically reduced, not because there have been fewer disastrous events, but because governments have taken action to prepare for disasters and reduce risks. While Cyclone Sidr killed around 3,000 people in Bangladesh in 2007, this was a tiny fraction of the numbers killed by Cyclone Bhola in 1972 or even by Cyclone Gorky in 1991, despite the fact that these storms were similar in strength or weaker. In countries like India, where the National Rural Employment Guarantee Act has created 900 million person-days of employment for rural people living in poverty, the advent of social protection mechanisms offers at least the hope that the cycle of disaster and poverty can be broken.[14] In Chile in May 2008, the eruption of Mount Chaitén – the first in recorded history – was met with a speedy response, including the deployment of civil defence teams and the evacuation of 8,000 people.[15]

State responsibility

As with any human right, the state is the principal guarantor of its citizens' right to life. And the impetus to make the state deliver better life-saving assistance is often the action of citizens holding their governments to account. In Indonesia, Oxfam works with Flores Integrated Rural Development (FIRD), a local organisation working in disaster management and response. Their mediation between local villages and the district government has helped to transform the delivery of aid. Dr Syrip Tintin of FIRD explains:

> Before, the district government would have to go and give support [to local communities] in distributing relief. But now they are the ones who come to the district government and say 'we are ready; what can you do next?'.[16]

In conflict as well as disasters, civil-society organisations can influence the way affected people are treated, and support them in demanding that governments uphold their rights. In August 2008, up to 130,000 people were displaced in Georgia, in and around the disputed regions of South Ossetia and Abkhazia. Organisations like the Georgian Young Lawyers Association played a vital role in ensuring that those affected knew what help they were entitled to, and that the national authorities provided it.[17]

> Many displaced people do not know how to register, nor do they know of their rights... We are giving legal aid and providing legal representation to people affected.

Besarion Boxasvili (GYLA)[18]

But for every government that acts to protect lives in the face of threats such as storms and conflict, there are far too many that fail. Sometimes this is because they are simply overwhelmed by the weight of disasters. Even Cuba, one of the countries best prepared for disasters, failed to prevent tropical storm-related deaths in 2008, following four successive hurricanes. But others fail through choice. Governments often blame their failure to invest in disaster preparedness on economic constraints. But the fact that some poor states have implemented successful measures to reduce the risk of disasters shows that this is no adequate excuse.

Some governments actively abuse their own citizens or those of occupied territories. Others, as well as some non-state actors, are complicit in the deliberate manipulation and denial of humanitarian aid. In 2007, UN Secretary-General Ban Ki-moon reported that conflict was limiting or preventing humanitarian access to over 18 million people in countries like Iraq, Somalia, Sudan, and Afghanistan either due to general insecurity or deliberate obstruction.[19]

International assistance

International aid organisations play a crucial role, both in acting directly to save lives where governments fail, and working to support governments that choose to act responsibly. Humanitarian organisations, both local and international, regularly demonstrate enormous skill, commitment and courage in delivering essential aid to those who need it most, in countries from Chad to Burma/Myanmar. In 2007, more than 43 million people benefited from humanitarian assistance provided under UN appeals.[20] In November 2008, Oxfam was directly assisting 3.3 million people with humanitarian needs.[21]

In 2007 in Bolivia, Oxfam worked alongside local government agencies to quickly and effectively respond to serious floods, and to adapt the agricultural system to cope with regular flooding and drought, to improve soil fertility, and make the land productive. The construction of elevated seedbeds, *camellones*, now prevents seasonal floodwater destroying food crops.[22]

But too often, international humanitarian agencies pay scant regard to working with national or local governments (or with local civil-society organisations, such as national Red Cross and Red Crescent Societies). In pursuing the 'default' option of providing assistance directly, international organisations too often give the impression that they are absolving governments of their obligations and reducing the likelihood of basic services being restored in the future. That is not to say that international humanitarian organisations should never act directly to save lives – rather, that working through government and civil-society partners is preferable where it is feasible.

Too much humanitarian aid is still inappropriate and poorly targeted. Too often, humanitarian assistance does not take account of the specific needs of different groups, like women and men for instance. The vulnerability of women and girls to sexual violence, for example, may actually be increased by poorly designed aid projects. Nor is the humanitarian system well set up to deal with the increasing number of local climate disasters. In the past, traditional responses to large-scale catastrophes have often been centralised, logistics-heavy interventions. In the future, humanitarian organisations will need to focus more on building local capacity to help prevent, prepare for, and respond to this proliferation of climate-related shocks.

The current level of humanitarian funding is still far too low to meet even today's humanitarian needs. The world spent more on video games in 2006 than it did on international humanitarian assistance.[23] The significant amount of aid already coming from non-OECD humanitarian donors, from the Middle East and elsewhere, should also of course be increased.

The issue is not just one of quantity, however. Too much money, from OECD and non-OECD donors alike, is allocated according to the political or security interests of governments – or according to whichever disaster is on the television screens of each country – rather than impartially on the basis of humanitarian need. Comparing the global response to the Indian Ocean tsunami in 2004 with the response to the conflict in Chad in the same year, the 500,000 people assisted after the tsunami received an average of $1,241 each in official aid, while the 700,000 recipients of aid in Chad received just $23 each.[24]

Building a safer future

The humanitarian challenge of the twenty-first century is this: an increasing total of largely local catastrophic events, increasing numbers of people vulnerable to them, too many governments failing to prevent or respond to them, and an international humanitarian system unable to cope. In the face of that, disaster-affected people need:

- A far greater focus on building national governments' capacity to respond to disasters – and, where needed, challenging those governments to use it;
- A far greater focus on helping people, and national governments, to become less vulnerable to disasters; and
- An international humanitarian system that acts quickly and impartially to provide effective and accountable assistance – complementing national capacity, and sometimes providing the aid that national governments fail to.

That will require the following:

Building state responsibility and empowering affected people

- Governments must reinforce national and local capacity to respond in emergencies and to reduce people's vulnerability; donor governments and others must substantially increase their support to help them do that;
- Communities must be empowered to demand that governments and others fulfil their obligations to safeguard their lives, as well as to respond to and prepare for disasters themselves; and
- The international community, including regional organisations, must use mediation and diplomacy far more robustly to press states to assist their own citizens.

Reducing vulnerability

- National governments must:
  - Adopt disaster risk-reduction measures combining early warning, preparedness plans, effective communication, and grassroots community mobilisation;
  - Invest in sustainable livelihoods so that people have secure incomes and food;
  - Improve urban planning so that people living in slums are housed in more disaster-resistant dwellings and in areas that are less subject to environmental risk; and
  - Invest in public services and infrastructure so that public-health risks are reduced.
- All parties must take assertive and effective action to reduce conflicts. This is the subject of a companion Oxfam report, 'For a Safer Tomorrow', which contains detailed recommendations;[25] and
- In line with their responsibility (for causing climate change) and their capability (to pay), rich country governments must lead in cutting global emissions so that global warming stays as far below a 2°C global average temperature increase as possible, and provide at least $50bn per year to help poor countries adapt to climate change; see the Oxfam Briefing Paper, 'Climate Wrongs and Human Rights'.[26]

Improving international assistance

- Governments, donors, the UN, and humanitarian agencies must ensure that humanitarian needs are properly assessed; and that aid is implemented impartially, according to need, and to appropriate international standards, accountable to its beneficiaries, sensitive to particular vulnerabilities (including by gender, age, and disability), and supporting and building on local capacity wherever possible;
- Donor governments and others must substantially increase their support to developing country governments to reduce vulnerability to disasters;
- Non-OECD donors must follow the same standards as OECD ones, to provide aid in the above way; OECD donors should do much more to include non-OECD donors in their co-ordination mechanisms;
- UN agencies must provide better leadership and co-ordination of the international humanitarian response. Individual NGO and UN organisations must support a more co-ordinated international response, supportive of national authorities, while preserving their independence; and
- Donors must work much more closely together to ensure that there is adequate funding to support timely, effective, and good-quality humanitarian action. Increasing humanitarian aid to $42bn a year would be a vital first step.

NASA

Tropical Cyclone Sidr moves towards the Bangladesh coast, 14 November 2007. The coast of western Bangladesh, the most densely populated low-lying area in the world, has seen some of the worst human disasters of recent decades. Cyclone Sidr claimed the lives of some 3,000 people, yet many hundreds of thousands more were evacuated to safety.

Introduction

The growing threat

Humanitarian emergencies caused by conflict, other human-made crises, and environmental hazards cause immense suffering. For those who do not immediately lose their lives, many will lose loved ones, experience catastrophic damage to their homes and livelihoods, witness the destruction of their communities, and suffer the dangers and humiliations of displacement and destitution. For them, the aftermath of a catastrophe becomes a daily struggle for survival, for dignity and for a future. This is the reality now for over a quarter of a billion women and men a year.[27]

As the twenty-first century progresses, humanity will face a greater threat from catastrophic events. In this report, we estimate the growth in humanitarian need between now and 2015 and look at some of the reasons why so many more people will feel the impact of these catastrophic events in the coming decades. In particular, we look at how vulnerability, defined by who one is, where one lives, and how one makes a living, will have a direct bearing on the chances of surviving the immediate effects or longer-term impact of catastrophes with health and livelihood intact.

This report asks what can realistically be done to help those affected by the vast and seemingly overwhelming forces of climate change, population growth, displacement, and vulnerability. We will demonstrate that the necessary skills, knowledge, and financial resources can be mobilised to radically reduce the numbers of people who will die or be made destitute by catastrophes. But for this to happen, all parties – governments, the UN, civil-society organisations, and ordinary citizens – must acknowledge and respond to the growing threat. Whether or not there is sufficient will to do this will be one of the defining features of our age, and will dictate whether millions live or die.

Mirlene Chery, 9, learns songs and role-plays about reducing risks from disasters. As part of its disaster risk reduction work in Haiti, Oxfam works with school children and teachers to alert them to the danger of natural disasters and how they can keep themselves and their families safe (2007).

Abbie Trayler-Smith/Oxfam GB

From charity to entitlement

The world has the means at its disposal both to prevent and mitigate current and future threats arising from catastrophic events. So rather than seeing those who die or are made homeless and destitute by catastrophes as passive victims of natural disasters, we should see them as sufferers of a grave failure to safeguard the most basic of human rights, the right to life.

Furthermore, as the threats from global forces such as climate change, population movements, and displacement grow, and as the world begins to see a proliferation of localised, climate-driven emergencies, who is best placed to guarantee this right to life? Who needs to be enabled to respond in emergencies and to reduce vulnerability to them in the long term?

As with any human right, national governments are the principal guarantors of their citizens' right to life. Guaranteeing that right depends on two principal things. First, effective and accountable states must take responsibility for reducing the number of preventable deaths in emergencies. They must do so by investing in effective civil defence, early warning and communications that will allow them to respond in emergencies, as well as investing in long-term measures to reduce their citizens' vulnerability to shocks. This may be beyond the capability of some states – failed states, states with limited capacity, or those simply overwhelmed by the scale of needs. But most governments are in a position to make this choice, as positive examples of successful adaptation by poor states like Cuba have shown. Second, active citizens must demand assistance, and long-term changes to reduce their vulnerability, from local authorities and other aid providers –– and take them to task when they fail to provide it.

But if governments are the principal guarantors of the right to assistance, where does this leave international humanitarian organisations? What is the responsibility of the UN, regional multilateral bodies, or indeed local civil-society organisations? The late twentieth (and early twenty-first) century, with its succession of conflicts, failed states, and mega-emergencies, created a humanitarian aid system that, at its best, sought to protect human life through rigorous impartial and independent action. But it also created a system, predominantly Western-based, that thrived on centralised responses to large, high-profile disasters. Many of these responses paid scant regard to working with national governments or

A sign hangs from a balcony of a home in Gulfport, Mississippi, USA. The residents lived through the landfall of Hurricane Katrina (August 2005).

Jim Reed/Getty Images

with local civil-society organisations. Little attention beyond lip-service was paid until relatively recently to treating those affected by disasters as anything other than the passive recipients of welfare.

A new humanitarian framework

If the world is to respond to the growing and evolving threats that will characterise the twenty-first century, a new, more effective global humanitarian framework is required. A system is needed whose primary focus is to support states in their efforts to reduce risks and respond effectively in emergencies; a system that reinforces *both* states' responsibilities to provide assistance *and* citizens' capacity to claim it. This twenty-first century humanitarianism must combine the best of the twentieth-century humanitarian system and its principles of humanity and impartiality with an approach rooted in the rights of those affected by emergencies. It must be more accountable to them, more localised and less centralised, and deliver not just an excellent response to emergencies, but effective action to reduce the risk of disasters as well.

International humanitarian organisations must work better with both states and local civil-society organisations to prepare for emergencies. More resources need to be devoted to reducing the risks of long-term food insecurity and environmental threats such as flooding, tropical storms, and earthquakes. Local civil-society organisations need to be imbued with the confidence and capacity to challenge failures on behalf of those affected by emergencies.

Many governments will still fail to provide adequate assistance to their own people, either through incapacity, or through wilful negligence or deliberate obstruction. With this in mind, multilateral organisations must place pressure on non-compliant states to fulfil their obligations, or – where this fails – to facilitate rapid and unimpeded access by international humanitarian agencies.

Jane Beesley / Oxfam

'When we hear the weather forecast, we can warn the community to prepare.' Shahia, chair of a Oxfam-supported disaster preparedness group in Bangladesh, listens out for flood alerts on the radio. When the floods of 2007 struck, villages with emergency committees were better prepared to deal with the disaster. Many belongings and livestock were saved, and nobody died (2007).

Our future to choose

At the beginning of the twenty-first century, it is possible to address every affected person's humanitarian need. Even in times of economic crisis, it is still possible to take effective action. It does not follow that, simply because climate-related threats are likely to increase at a time when governments may have less to spend, more people have to die or be made destitute as a result.

In Chapter 2, we look at the growing threat to life and livelihood posed by catastrophic events and by human vulnerability derived from poverty, inequality, and powerlessness. In Chapter 3, we ask how governments can guarantee the right to life in emergencies, and explore what is required from international humanitarian agencies to help them. In Chapter 4, we explore exactly how international humanitarian assistance can become more strategic, more locally based, and more accountable. In Chapter 5, we look at the long-term issues that cause lives and livelihoods to be lost in emergencies, and the solutions to them. In Chapter 6, we look at how much all this will cost – and how it can be paid for. We show that these needs can be met: by today's rich countries and by seizing the opportunities from the growing number of humanitarian donors from the global South. And we show how new humanitarian actors, acting impartially and according to best-practice standards, can help ensure that this money gets to where it is most needed. Finally, in Chapter 7, we bring all these issues together and make recommendations for how the right to assistance can be guaranteed by responsible states, active citizens, and a more effective global humanitarian framework.

'We used to say, "It's better to be with a neighbour than with a brother", but when your neighbour is your enemy ... you can't go back,' Joshua, displaced by election violence, Kenya, April 2008.

Jane Beesley / Oxfam GB

2

New threats and old

Wars and violence affect millions of people every year, driving them from their homes and destroying their livelihoods. And there is some evidence that the number of conflicts, which fell dramatically after the end of the Cold War, is once again on the rise.[28]

In the Democratic Republic of Congo (DRC), two people died every minute from the country's shamefully neglected conflict, according to figures published in 2008.[29] That is equal to a disaster the size of an Indian Ocean tsunami striking the country every six months.[30] Since 1998, more than 5.4 million people have died in the DRC as a result of the conflict, but less than 1 per cent of those have been killed by fighting.[31] The vast majority succumbed to preventable communicable diseases, such as malaria and diarrhoea. Such diseases were commonplace because of the conflict's devastating effect on the public-health infrastructure. In 2007, 57 per cent of the population had no access to safe drinking water and 54 per cent lacked access to medical services.[32] The upsurge in violence in the second half of 2008 was a painful reminder that even the most protracted conflicts can get worse, and create hundreds of thousands more people who are displaced or in need of humanitarian aid.

Conflict is not confined to 'failed' states like the DRC. Events in 2008 demonstrated that even outwardly stable societies are vulnerable to conflict. The disputed elections in Kenya exposed underlying political tensions and led to an outpouring of violence. More than 1,000 people died, and at least 500,000 people were displaced. Tens of thousands sought asylum in neighbouring countries.[33] Such upheavals have a huge impact on the lives of those affected, long after the original crisis has slipped from the headlines. For Joshua, displaced with his family from Kenya's Nandi Hills region, it was clear he would not go home in the near future:

> Even if we went back the people there wouldn't accept us. When the trouble started we lost everything we had. This was the place where we had our livelihoods, where we had our jobs, our homes, where we brought up our families. We lived with people – our neighbours – for years, people we thought were our friends. Now they'd kill us. We cannot return.[34]

— Pegu

Bassein

— Yangon

Moulmein —

Mouths of the Irrawaddy

Gulf of Martaban

N 25 km

April 15, 2008

— Pegu

Bassein

Yangon

Moulmein —

May 5, 2008
NASA

Satellite images of the Burma/
Myanmar coast before and after
the devastation of flooding
caused by Tropical Cyclone
Nargis in May 2008.

22

Kenya was only one of 27 countries under the most acute pressure, and consequent risk of conflict or state failure, identified in one study published in November 2008.[35] Others ranged from Pakistan to Haiti. While it is impossible to predict where future conflicts will break out, or whether the total number of conflicts will rise or fall, there is a wide range of risks that could lead to increased insecurity in the next ten years and beyond. Some risks are associated with major global trends, such as climate change, continuing poverty and inequality, and growing population in 'youth-bulge' states. Others are associated with events that, though not probable, are possible, including the terrorist use of weapons of mass destruction. In short, conflict-driven humanitarian needs are likely to remain substantial, and could increase.

The upward trend of natural disasters is, however, easier to identify. Already they exact a huge toll in human suffering. In a year of climate crisis, 2007 saw floods in 23 African and 11 Asian countries that were the worst for decades. Two hurricanes and heavy rains hit much of Central America; almost half the state of Tabasco in Mexico was flooded.[36] As the UN Emergency Relief Coordinator John Holmes put it: '...all these events on their own didn't have massive death tolls, but if you add [them] together you get a mega-disaster'.[37] But 2008 offered no let-up in the barrage of climatic disasters, as Cyclone Nargis devastated large parts of Burma/Myanmar, and a particularly destructive Atlantic hurricane season caused hundreds of deaths and massive economic damage across Cuba, the Dominican Republic, Haiti, and the USA. In many cases, failures in environmental management massively increased the impact of these climate hazards. In India, the 2008 rains caused serious flooding, not because they were particularly heavy, but because of the failure of poorly maintained dams and river banks.[38] A breach in the Kosi river embankment in August 2008 led to one of the worst floods in the history of Bihar, the poorest state in India. Tarzamul Haq, a farm labourer from Kataiya village, was forced to move his family to a relief camp near the Nepal border. Tarzamul saw his livestock and crops washed away by the floods.

> I have no money and all the grains I had saved...have been washed away. The landlord himself has lost all his crops and belongings so he cannot help. The flood water will take time to recede and at least two crops...will be lost. How will I feed my family?

In 2008, over 3.8 million people were affected by the floods in Bihar and more than 100,000 hectares of cultivable land were inundated. It will take

A rising tide of suffering: The growth in numbers of people affected by climate-related disasters 1980–2007 with forecast to 2015

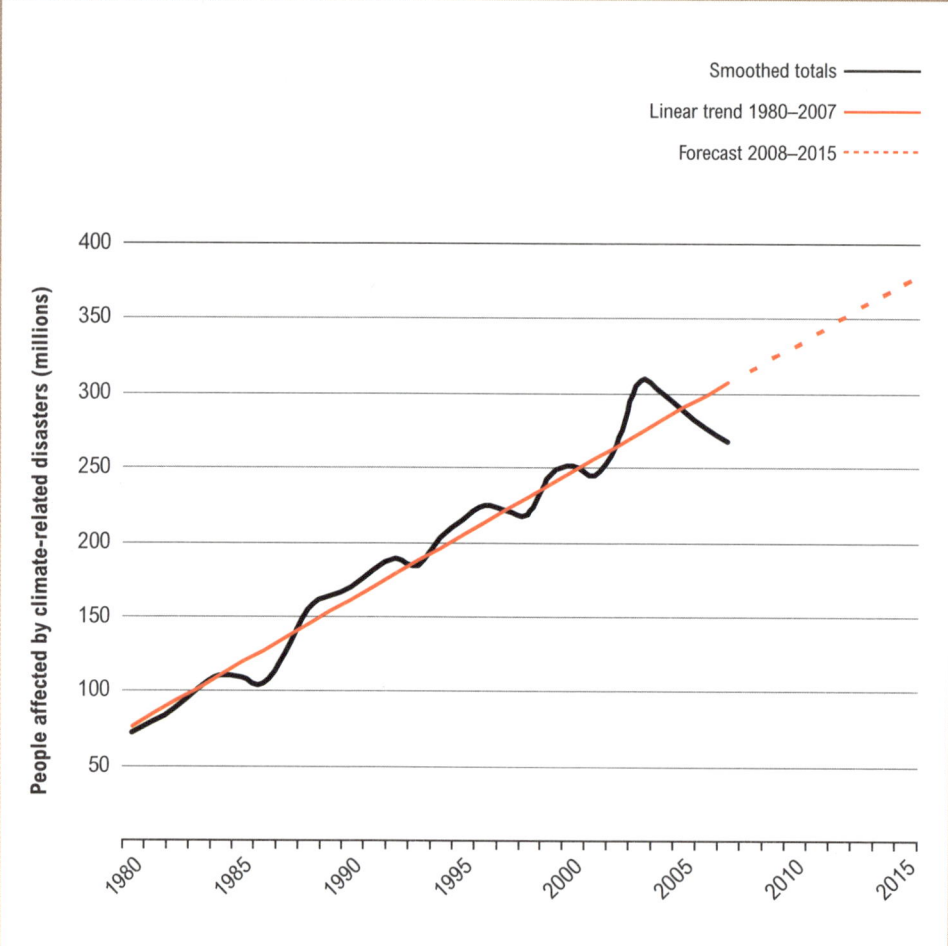

Source: Centre for Research on the Epidemiology of Disasters (CRED) Emergency Database (EM-DAT), http://www.emdat.be

The climate-related hazards data recorded in CRED shows a significant variation in the number of people affected from one year to another, reflecting a number of very large natural disasters. Oxfam's analysis has used a statistical 'smoothing' technique to even out the extreme highs and lows in the data and show a clearer underlying trend. This chart shows a smoothed trend series estimated from the original CRED data using Double Exponential Smoothing (with a smoothing weight equivalent to using 112 quarters). A linear regression forecast model is modelled on that smoothed data. For more details of the methodology, results, and limitations of these projections, please see 'Forecasting the numbers of people affected annually by natural disasters up to 2015', www.oxfam.org.uk.

years for people like Tarzamul to recover the losses that they incurred. Poor maintenance of infrastructure, deforestation in upland areas, erosion, silting, rising riverbeds, and changing river courses mean that, for hundreds of thousands of people in India, such devastating floods are now a regular threat.

In the same year, hurricanes in the Atlantic showed that a number of disasters, hitting in close succession, could devastate poor countries. Haiti was hit by four storms in less than a month, leaving hundreds of thousands homeless and unable to meet their basic needs.[39]

In the meantime, often away from the world's gaze, large populations in East and Central Africa and South Asia grow ever more vulnerable to an annual cycle of drought. In 2008, the failure of rains in Ethiopia left millions of people in need of food aid.[40] For millions of the world's poorest people, it is this relentless attrition of cyclical disasters that erodes their ability to cope.

According to new research for this report, by 2015 there may be more than a 50 per cent increase in the numbers of people affected by climate-related disasters in an average year compared with the decade 1998–2007, bringing the yearly average to more than 375 million people.[41] This projected increase could overwhelm the world's current capacity to respond.

Globalisation: the impact of food prices

Although the number of localised disasters is growing, people are also increasingly likely to experience shocks that are truly global in scope. The global crisis in food prices that peaked in 2008 was the result of a complex interrelated series of factors, crossing state and regional borders. These include a soaring oil price, and the large-scale production of biofuels, driven by demand in the European Union and USA, which increased demand for food crops (while doing little, if anything, to reduce carbon emissions). Other factors included the long-term failure of donor and Southern governments to invest in small-scale agriculture, and the continued hardship caused to poor farmers by rich-world agricultural policies. All played their part in creating a global crisis which threatened to cause political insecurity, as well as pushing vulnerable countries already affected by chronic undernourishment towards acute humanitarian crisis.[42]

Children play in a gulley caused by erosion after strong rains and floods in Vicus, northwest Peru. Like many places in the area, Vicus is prone to flooding and landslides. Oxfam and its partner Centro Ideas are supporting the local civil defence committee to be better prepared for disasters (2008).

Climate change

It was dark when the water came. The wave was higher than the house. People clung to the highest trees to survive, while our village was swallowed up. So many people died – I lost my son, he was nearly four. My only brother and both of my sisters are gone. Our homes are gone too, and everything in them, even our clothes.

Mahmouda, Ketasara village, Bangladesh, describing the force of Cyclone Sidr, 2007[43]

Mahmouda was one of hundreds of millions of people whose lives were devastated by flooding and storms across three continents in 2007. For them, the world's changing climate is already a deadly reality. Comparing the century and a half before with the ten years after 1996, the average number of tropical storms per decade in the north Atlantic has risen by 40 per cent. The average number of Atlantic hurricanes per year, comparing the same two periods, has increased from five to eight.[44] The severity of tropical storms is also thought to be increasing. The Inter-governmental Panel on Climate Change (IPCC) states that it is 'likely' that tropical cyclones will become more destructive, as tropical sea-surface temperatures continue to rise.[45]

While the fury of tropical storms will have sudden and catastrophic effects on vulnerable communities, the more insidious consequences of climate change, such as water scarcity and gradual sea-level rises brought about by rising temperatures, will play no less a role in generating humanitarian need. Global sea-level rises will leave many of the 200 million people who live on the world's coastal floodplains (35 million of them in Bangladesh alone) vulnerable to displacement and destruction of homes and livelihoods. Longer warm seasons may contribute to an increase in transmission of communicable diseases, such as malaria. A climate model produced by the UK Meteorological Office predicts that, by 2080, 30 per cent of the earth's surface will be subject to extreme drought, compared with 3 per cent at the beginning of the twenty-first century.[46]

More localised disasters

The frequency of disasters has been growing for the past 30 years.[47] This has been driven by a marked increase since the mid 1990s in climate-related shocks (cyclones and, to a lesser degree, floods).[48] These multiple climatic shocks will strike hard at particular communities and regions and will cause immense human suffering on a global scale. 'Mega-disasters'– like

Binyam Mengesha / PANOS

'It is during acute droughts that we enter into conflict with other clans.' Chuqulisa, Borena, southern Ethiopia.

Since the late 1980s, pastureland and water sources in Borena have been destroyed by drought and desertification. Partly as a result of this, conflict has intensified between the Boran and the Digodi pastoralists. (2007)

the Indian Ocean tsunami, which affect hundreds of thousands or even millions of people – may continue to cause the majority of disaster-related deaths, but the *growth* in numbers of people affected is likely to come as a result of these smaller, climate-related emergencies.[49] Disasters, like the floods and landslides that hit the Philippines in February 2008 (which affect particular regions or even lone communities and cause relatively low mortality in each individual crisis), will together contribute towards a considerable rise in the numbers killed and affected every year. In the face of this growing and proliferating threat, traditional humanitarian response – centralised, logistics-heavy, and geared towards big emergencies – will be too expensive and cumbersome to be effective. Local government, civil society, and community-based institutions will often be much better placed to respond.

Climate change driving conflict

The impact of climate change will not just be confined to natural disasters and gradual shifts in weather patterns or sea levels. Globally, traditional drivers of violent conflict will be made all the more potent by the impact of climate change. One study has suggested that climate change will place 46 countries – home to 40 per cent of the world's population – at increased risk of being affected by violent conflict.[50] Across sub-Saharan Africa, Central and South Asia and the Middle East, some suggest we have already seen such an increase in climate-aggravated conflict. In Darfur, long-standing local conflict was certainly made worse by increasing scarcity of water and pasture.[51] But it was the exploitation of these tensions in the struggle for political power in Sudan that greatly exacerbated the conflict. Environmental change was cruelly mishandled, so that some groups suffered far more than others, and tensions increased.

But climate-related threats – along with geological shocks, conflict, and other threats – are only part of the picture. Vulnerability – the combination of factors that place certain people at greater risk from threats – will determine whether people survive and prosper in a changing world. People's *growing* vulnerability to disasters over the coming decades will be a crucial component of the humanitarian challenge.

'Suddenly we heard a noise…the embankment was breached and the water flooded towards our houses,' Balkru Behera (left) with his father, Nanda, Orissa, India (2007).

Vulnerability and poverty

Suddenly we heard a noise...the embankment was breached and the water flooded towards our houses. We just managed to save our lives, but not the household contents or our domestic animals...the water washed them all away. For two days we lived in complete fear...all the time the break in the embankment was slowly increasing as the river took it away. Some of us still had some polythene sheets from the [1999] super cyclone; around four families sat under one sheet, just holding on to it with our hands whilst it was raining.

There was no food for days. After four days a local institution came with the local minister and gave out food relief.

Balkru Behera, Orissa, India, 2007[52]

The severe rains that devastated much of Orissa and West Bengal in June 2007 became a threat to Balkru's life and home because his community was particularly vulnerable to flooding. Poverty makes millions like Balkru more vulnerable to being killed or made destitute by disasters. Poor people are more likely to live in densely populated areas, in poorly constructed and poorly sited housing; more likely too to suffer the effects of falling land productivity, lack of savings, insecure land tenure, and lack of access to health care. Poor people are also more likely to live in parts of the world affected by conflict.

Exposure to the effects of disasters and conflict also increases poverty and vulnerability. This deadly feedback loop between poverty, vulnerability, and disaster, if ignored over the coming decades, will exact an ever-greater toll in lives lost and livelihoods shattered. With the exception of droughts, death rates per disaster show a clear upward trend in every part of the world – evidence that vulnerability to most kinds of climatic disasters is increasing.[53] Again, it is poor people who are most at risk. In rich countries, the average number of deaths per disaster is 23, while in the poorest countries this average is 1,052.[54] When the great Hanshin earthquake, measuring 7.3 on the Richter scale, struck Japan in 1995, it claimed the lives of some 6,000 people – the worst disaster to afflict the country in decades. But in 2005, the Kashmir earthquake in Pakistan, measuring 7.6 on the Richter scale, claimed 75,000 lives – 12 times as many – despite the fact that the earthquake affected areas with much lower population density.[55] The inequitable burden of disasters will continue to be felt within nations as well as between them. The impact of Hurricane Katrina on New Orleans, one of the poorest cities in the world's richest country, fell hardest on its poorest

Jane Beesley / Oxfam GB

Hawa (80), a refugee from fighting in Darfur, arrived in Chad on a donkey after travelling for 8 nights. Unwilling to talk about the journey, she said 'things are better now. We have water, and … the Oxfam latrine has made our lives much easier. Before, we [women] had to walk very far to hide from the men'. Identifying and responding to specific vulnerabilities and needs such as gender and age are fundamental responsibilities for humanitarian agencies (2005).

residents. In the widespread political and public outrage that followed Katrina, it appeared to many that the difference between who lived and who died was perhaps 'nothing more than poverty, age or skin colour'.[56]

For some groups – elderly people, women and girls, chronically ill people – their identity may mean that they are even more vulnerable to the effects of disaster, because their ability to cope may be limited by discrimination, their traditional roles, or their physical health. Where food is scarce, for instance, pregnant and breastfeeding mothers may be at additional risk, not only because of their nutritional needs, but because their mobility may be restricted by child-care responsibilities or limited by cultural convention. In conflict, men are frequently at risk from forced recruitment or targeted killings, while women are vulnerable to rape and sexual assault. In a refugee camp in Darfur, a male resident explains the terrible inevitability of the choice facing families: 'You might have someone sick...but you can't [go] because when you come from your shelter you might meet an armed person – a man with a gun, who might attack you...We can't do anything about this. We are powerless...our women are going out every night to spend the night at the water points to wait for water. [They] are waiting three days and three nights to fill their jerry cans.' Asked if that isn't dangerous for the women, he replies with a gesture of desperation, 'Yes! It is! But it's the only option. What can we do?'[57]

The risks facing particular categories of people cut across the many global factors driving vulnerability. But in a future characterised by a significant growth in the number of catastrophic events, where and how people live – as well as who they are – will be critical in determining whether they live or die. In the rest of this chapter, we examine three key factors in vulnerability: population density, vulnerable livelihoods, and displacement.

Rising population density and urban poverty

By 2025, indications are that the global population will increase from 6.6 billion to 8 billion people, with 99 per cent of that growth occurring in developing countries.[58] Over 5 billion people will by that point live in urban areas, 2 billion of whom will be squeezed into overcrowded and poorly planned urban slums.[59]

Where poverty and population density collide, vulnerability to catastrophes increases. In urban areas, the problem is principally one of finding safe housing within a finite space and with limited resources. As

West Point, Monrovia, Liberia. Built on a low-lying coastal peninsula vulnerable to flooding, West Point is home to approximately 65,000 people, who live in cramped and unsanitary conditions (2007).

Aubrey Wade / Oxfam GB

urban populations swell, poor people are often forced to build their homes in areas prone to landslips and flash flooding. Due to lack of resources and insecure tenure, the houses that they build are often of poor quality.

Mumbai is one of the world's most populous cities. Built on a narrow, low-lying promontory jutting into the Arabian Sea, it is also one of the most vulnerable cities in the world to coastal and rainwater flooding. Some 54 per cent of the city's population live in slums, many of them built on reclaimed swampland to the north and east of the centre. In July 2005, widespread flooding in Mumbai caused the deaths of around 900 people, most killed not by drowning but by landslips and collapsed buildings.[60] The impact of unusually high rainfall was compounded by failure to invest in replacing Mumbai's crumbling early twentieth-century drainage network, the uncontrolled development of the city's poorer suburbs, and the destruction of rainwater sinks (in particular, the mangrove swamps that had once surrounded the city).[61]

Sudden shocks such as flooding and earthquakes are not the only risks for poor urban populations. People live close to each other, without adequate housing, water and sanitation, health services, or education, leading to the increased risk of epidemics of communicable disease.[62] And poor people in urban settings are often highly vulnerable to conflict and violence too. Urban growth often coincides with increased armed violence, driven by factors such as the drug trade, the availability of guns and organised crime.[63] But in poor countries, such violence is as often political as it is criminal. As armed groups are mobilised to oppose or maintain power, urban violence can rapidly escalate with devastating consequences for civilian populations, as events in both Kenya and Haiti in 2008 demonstrated.[64]

The growing insecurity of rural livelihoods

In rural areas, high population density, the increasing stress on productive land, soil degradation, and increasing aridity due to climate change are making hundreds of millions of rural livelihoods vulnerable. People are being forced to eke out a precarious living on land that is becoming more and more arid and degraded, with the result that food is getting harder and harder to come by.

The overwhelmingly rural population of Eastern Hararghe in Ethiopia is growing by 3 per cent every year, creating huge pressure on available land

A camp for internally displaced people near Goma , DRC, June 2008.

Suzi O'Keefe / Oxfam

and water resources. Massive deforestation and the cultivation of unsuitable slopes and hilltops have led to soil erosion and degradation, further reducing the amount of cultivatable land available. The size of many family holdings has shrunk, as plots are subdivided among children. Many families in the region are unable, even in years of bumper harvest, to meet their basic food needs, leaving them chronically undernourished and dependent on food aid. In years when crops fail, whether due to drought or heavy rains, the likelihood of dying or becoming sick due to malnutrition increases significantly, particularly among vulnerable groups such as children, pregnant women, nursing mothers, and elderly people.[65]

Under such circumstances, rural households are forced to sell off an ever-depleting pool of productive assets, bringing families closer to destitution. As Tabane explained following a period of acute drought in Ethiopia:

> *Everything has gone…died, worn out…anything left, I've had to sell. Every asset I had has gone. Now I don't even have clothes – just the ones you see. These clothes I'm wearing are also my nightclothes. The whole problem is because of the lack of rain.*[66]

Chronic undernourishment itself makes people more vulnerable to disasters. Not having enough to eat erodes an individual's health, leaving them at higher risk of dying when exposed to sudden shocks such as droughts, flooding, or violence. The UN Food and Agriculture Organization estimated that in 2007 there were 923 million undernourished people worldwide, with this number set to increase.[67] A quarter of undernourished people in the world live in India. Some Indian government estimates indicate that half of all India's children are malnourished.[68] In sub-Saharan Africa, one in three people don't have enough to eat. In 2006, some 48 per cent of children in Uganda were stunted because of food scarcity, largely due to 20 years of internal armed conflict.[69]

Forced displacement

> *The day war broke out, I didn't have time to collect anything from my house. There was shooting everywhere. The only things you had with you were what you had on from early morning.*

Esperance, eastern Democratic Republic of Congo, 2004[70]

It is hard to overstate how dangerous, alienating, and humiliating the experience of forced displacement is. The destruction of homes, separation from family, the loss of access to productive assets (land, livestock, seed

'We're doing a lot more things to prepare and cope with floods than we used to,' Darius Gare, coordinator of a village emergency response team, with a risk map of their village (Indonesia, 2008).

Jane Beesley / Oxfam GB

stocks), lack of access to water and hygiene items, the loss of personal effects such as clothing – all combine to generate huge vulnerability.

In 2008, the UN High Commissioner for Refugees (UNHCR) estimated that there are 67 million people in the world who have been forced to flee from their homes because of conflict or disasters. Of these, some 11.4 million had been forced to flee to another country as refugees, while another 51 million were internally displaced. UNHCR estimates that more than half the world's refugees now live in urban areas, a proportion that seems set to grow.[71]

The vulnerability of a displaced population to further shocks is naturally higher than for those who are able to maintain a settled life. Stripped of livelihoods, assets, and supportive networks, refugees and internally displaced people often find themselves requiring both protection (from ongoing violence, including sexual violence) and material assistance in order to survive. Yet states are often reluctant to provide assistance to displaced people, seeing them as a burden on public services, a potential challenge to the political status quo, or even a security threat.

In the next few decades, increasing and shifting populations and climate change will exacerbate existing problems such as conflict, food shortages, and land dispossession. This will lead to a significant growth in the numbers of those forced to leave their homes.[72] Some estimates suggest that that up to one billon people could be forcibly displaced between now and 2050.[73]

Choosing to act

We used to take it for granted that the floods would happen, and we did nothing about it…we thought it was just something from God and we had to live with it. Now we have the [emergency preparedness] team and we're more prepared to cope, we've built embankments and planted bamboos to strengthen the riverbanks, and we've identified locations in case we have to evacuate. We're doing a lot more things to prepare and cope with floods than we used to.

Darius Gare, village resident and elected co-ordinator of the village emergency team committee, Tanali, Flores, Indonesia, 2008[74]

There is no doubt that we live in a dangerous world. And there is no doubt that poor people are the most vulnerable to both conflict and natural disasters. But what are we doing about it *and what more should we be doing*? Beginning with the role of governments, the rest of this report addresses that question.

The right to humanitarian assistance in international law and custom

The two most important international legal instruments relating to those affected by humanitarian crises are the Universal Declaration of Human Rights and the Geneva Conventions. Neither contains a clearly stated 'right to humanitarian assistance'; nor a right to be protected from predictable threats like storms and floods. However, several authoritative interpretations of these and other key instruments of international law argue that people have a right to both these things. These interpretations include the UN Office for the Coordination of Humanitarian Affairs' Guiding Principles on Internal Displacement, the UN Inter-Agency Standing Committee's Operational Guidelines on Human Rights and Natural Disasters, The Code of Conduct for the International Red Cross and Red Crescent Movement and NGOs in Disaster Relief, and the Sphere Project Humanitarian Charter, developed by NGOs including Oxfam.[75]

The Universal Declaration of Human Rights

'Everyone has the right to life, liberty and security of person.' Article 3[76]

The Universal Declaration of Human Rights – and the binding conventions that flowed from it – conferred on all human beings a set of universal, indivisible, and inalienable rights, including the rights to life and security. It obliged states to respect human rights and to take the necessary steps to ensure their realisation.[77] They have a 'negative' duty not to infringe human rights and a 'positive' duty to proactively prevent their infringement.

States therefore have a duty to prevent and prepare for disasters that inevitably threaten the right to life.[78] As guarantors of that right, they are also obliged to take positive action to mitigate the effects of catastrophic events.[79] If states do not have the capacity to provide life-saving assistance themselves, this also implies they should allow third parties to do so. The UN Charter states that countries have a duty to co-operate with each other in 'solving international problems of [a]…humanitarian character'.

The Geneva Conventions: assistance and the law of conflict

'If the civilian population...is not adequately provided with [food, medical supplies, clothing, bedding, shelter and]...other supplies essential to the survival of the civilian population, relief actions which are humanitarian and impartial in character and conducted without any adverse distinctions shall be undertaken'.

Protocol I to the Geneva Conventions 1977[80]

The Geneva Conventions apply in situations of armed conflict. They oblige parties to conflict to distinguish between combatants and the civilian population at all times, and afford civilians – along with those no longer taking part in hostilities – special protection.

The Geneva Conventions and other aspects of international humanitarian law set out a series of rules for the humane treatment of civilians in conflict, summed up by one authoritative commentary in 2005.[81] The commentary includes that all parties (whether states or non-state actors such as insurgent groups) to all conflict (whether international or non-international in nature) are obliged to allow and facilitate rapid and unimpeded passage of humanitarian relief for civilians in need, subject to certain conditions: the destruction of infrastructure or services vital to survival (water supplies, medical facilities, etc.) is prohibited; the starvation of civilians as a method of warfare is forbidden;[82] and humanitarian relief personnel must be allowed freedom of movement (again, subject to conditions) and must be respected and protected.

Alexi and his family (foreground),
opened up their home to families
made homeless by violence in
Rutshuru, North Kivu, in the
Democratic Republic of Congo,
2008.

Robin Hammond / Guardian

3

Responsible governments and active citizens

The people from neighbouring villages, who hadn't been affected, would come here with food and clothes, and then about a month after the disaster had happened the government would finally come with food and clothes...It was never less than a month after the disaster.

Fransiskus, Indonesia, 2008[83]

When catastrophe strikes, it is often family and neighbours who are the first and most critical source of support to those who have been affected. Many people find sanctuary with family or friends, or in some cases complete strangers. In 2008, around 70 per cent of the 1.4 million internally displaced people in the DRC lived with host families, rather than in camps.[84]

Friends and family overseas can be as important a source of assistance as those closer to home. Data collected by the Overseas Development Institute in 2007 suggested that remittances were growing significantly as a source of support for families and communities in emergencies.[85]

Private companies and individuals, political parties, and civil-society groups all play key roles in providing life-saving aid to their communities in times of crisis. Indeed, in many cases, such organisations are the *only* source of assistance. In Burma/Myanmar in 2008, following Cyclone Nargis, religious institutions from all faiths in the Irrawaddy delta provided relief in the initial days following the disaster. Many ordinary Burmese citizens as well as businesses also responded, by clearing roads and waterways and donating water and food. Present in almost every country in the world, national Red Cross or Red Crescent Societies can play a key role, both in developing emergency-response skills and in providing response capacity. Following national emergencies, like the earthquake in Kyrgyzstan in October 2008, they are often among the first to provide outside help.[86]

Chinese President Hu Jintao
(centre) visits earthquake-
ravaged Beichuan in Sichuan
province, China (May 2008).

Paula Bronstein/Getty Images

Individuals, communities, and civil society respond spontaneously and generously to the needs of those affected by emergencies in contexts as diverse as the 2008 Sichuan earthquake in China, Hurricane Katrina in the USA in 2005, and, at the time of writing, the continuing political and economic crisis in Zimbabwe. They do so because bonds of kinship, personal morality, religious belief, or a sense of justice demands that they do so.

Assistance is a right

While individuals, families, and communities – local and global – may bear the burden of humanitarian assistance, it is governments who have the primary responsibility, both to safeguard life in the face of disasters and to build long-term human security (that is, security from all threats, whether they be environmental, epidemiological, or the result of conflict or extreme poverty).[87] See the box on pp 40–41.

In 1948, all the world's governments made a firm commitment – in the form of Article 3 of the Universal Declaration of Human Rights – to safeguard all people's rights to life and to security. But for human rights to have meaning, it is not enough for them simply to exist. In the aftermath of conflicts and disasters, affected communities are all too often left without the assistance required to save lives and protect livelihoods.

The political interest of states

If human rights – including the right to life – are to be realised, states have to recognise that it is in both their moral and political interest to act. Ultimately, governments are much more likely to act if they see a political benefit in effective response to unforeseen and catastrophic events. In fact, short of losing a war, appearing ineffective following national catastrophe can be the most politically damaging of failures.[88] Even superpowers are not immune to this effect. Some commentators have argued, for instance, that hesitancy and failure to acknowledge the scale of the 1986 Chernobyl nuclear accident undermined hardliners on the then Soviet Politburo, allowing Communist Party General Secretary Mikhail Gorbachev to seize the initiative and force through his key reforms of political openness (*glasnost*) and economic restructuring (*perestroika*) – with seismic political consequences.[89]

The response to Hurricane Katrina in 2005 was widely criticised in the USA as ineffective, and was a watershed in the presidency of George W. Bush. In a survey conducted for CBS News in the weeks after Katrina

How disaster risk reduction saves lives in Bangladesh

300,000 deaths
Cyclone Bhola
1971

138,000
Cyclone Gorky
1991

Cyclone Sidr
2007

3,000

Source: United Nations International Strategy for Disaster Reduction Secretariat (UNISDR)

Following a series of catastrophic storms in the 1970's, 1980's and 1990's, the Government of Bangladesh instituted a 48-hour early warning system, allowing people to evacuate to safe cyclone shelters before cyclones make landfall. This has drastically reduced the death tolls from cyclones.

struck, 65 per cent of Americans polled thought the Bush administration's response was inadequate.[90] While public approval ratings of the Bush Presidency's response to Hurricane Gustav and Hurricane Ike in 2008 were higher, there was still much criticism of the authorities' failure to adequately assist the poorest and most vulnerable people – in particular, those who were unable to self-evacuate from affected areas. Having received, in the aftermath of 9/11, the highest public approval rating ever recorded for a US president (over 90 per cent), after Hurricane Katrina, President Bush's job approval ratings never again rose above 42 per cent.[91]

But this pragmatic concern does not always mean that governments will act in their citizens' interest. If governments are to see a clear interest in saving lives, concerted and effective political pressure must be brought to bear by citizens.

The realisation of any human right lies in a combination of effective, accountable states and active citizens.[92] States must assist their citizens in the immediate aftermath of crisis, and reduce their long-term vulnerability to risk. Emergency-affected peoples must be empowered to demand adequate and timely assistance, and to hold their governments to account when they fail.

Responsible governments

The right of citizens to receive humanitarian assistance is clearly set out in the domestic laws of many modern states.[93] Almost inevitably, a successful national response to an emergency rarely makes international news. But this does not mean it hasn't been happening. In May 2008, Mount Chaitén in Chile erupted for the first time in its history. Despite the lack of warning, the government of Chile speedily deployed civil defence teams and evacuated 8,000 affected people. Emergency funding was quickly allocated and, with local water contaminated by ash, supplies of clean drinking water were trucked in.[94]

Government investment in emergency-response capacity and in mitigating the impact of disasters (known as disaster risk reduction) saves lives both in the short and long term. Cuba has proved its ability to minimise casualties in the face of (practically annual) hurricane strikes. As the International Federation of the Red Cross and Red Crescent reported, 'Cuba's success in saving lives through timely evacuation when Hurricane Michelle struck in November 2001 gives us a model of effective government-driven disaster

'I hid in the basement of my home for days. I cannot believe I am still alive.' Mzia, 75, was displaced by conflict in Georgia in 2008. During the conflict, the Georgian Young Lawyers Association (GYLA) worked to provide legal aid and representation to displaced people like Mzia, ensuring they were registered with the local authorities and knew their basic entitlements.

Marie Cacace / Oxfam GB

preparedness'.[95] Michelle claimed just five lives on the island after more than 700,000 people were evacuated to safety.[96]

Reducing the risks posed by disasters, a strategy we explore further in Chapter 5, is one way of reducing vulnerability to sudden shocks. Another way is to invest in 'social protection' mechanisms: entitling vulnerable groups (including poor, unemployed, and elderly people) to income support. India's National Rural Employment Guarantee Act (NREGA) was passed in 2005. Under it, each rural household has a right to 100 days of paid unskilled work per year on public-works projects. By 2008, the NREGA created 900 million person-days of employment for India's rural poor people. In a country which is home to a quarter of the world's undernourished population, the potential of the NREGA to reduce vulnerability to hunger is enormous.[97]

Climate change, through its impacts on risk and vulnerability, is undermining millions of people's fundamental human rights: rights to life, security, food, water, health and shelter, for example.[98] *Responsibility* for this global violation of human rights lies with the industrialised countries that became rich by burning fossil fuels over the last century, raising atmospheric CO_2 to current levels. Their greater wealth also means that it is these same countries that have the *capability* to respond.

This therefore creates two further obligations upon the governments of rich countries. First, they must bring these violations to an end as quickly as possible. This means avoiding so-called 'dangerous climate change' by making emissions cuts consistent with keeping increases in global average temperatures as far below 2°C as possible. Second, they must help those for whom it is too late, by providing funds to help poor countries adapt to climate change that is already unavoidable. Oxfam estimates that this requires at least $50bn a year, with much more needed unless emissions are cut rapidly.[99]

Active citizens

The NREGA came about because Indian national legislators had the political will to challenge rural vulnerability. With strong rights-based legislation and clear mechanisms of accountability, the NREGA has the potential to improve government services so that they meet the demands of active and empowered citizens.[100] Yet, in some Indian states, implementation of the NREGA has faced major obstacles, including

Sudan Liberation Army (SLA) soldiers patrol Gereida camp in a modified Toyota pick-up, South Darfur, Sudan (2007).

Sven Torfinn / Panos

corruption.[101] In the face of such challenges, the activism of citizens will be the key to allowing NREGA to realise its full potential. [102]

The impetus to deliver better assistance is often driven by citizens holding governments to account when they fail. In Indonesia, following the 2004 Indian Ocean tsunami, the immediate response from the government left many communities without adequate assistance. Oxfam supported community groups to use the UN's Guiding Principles on Internal Displacement to successfully lobby local government to improve their emergency provision. Oxfam works with Flores Integrated Rural Development (FIRD), an Indonesian partner working in disaster management and response. Their mediation between local villages and the district government helped transform the delivery of aid:

> Before, the district government would have to go and give support [to local communities] in distributing relief. But now they are the ones who come to the district government and say 'we are ready; what can you do next?'.

Dr Syrip Tintin, FIRD, 2008[103]

Failed states – and indifferent ones

The crucial issue is, of course, that many of the countries where people are most vulnerable to emergencies are precisely those where the bonds of accountability between state and citizen are weakest. Some states cite lack of financial resources for failing to invest in disaster preparedness or response. But many poor states have implemented successful disaster risk-reduction measures, which suggests that resources alone are not a deciding factor. Some states can seem to be indifferent to their citizens, and have other priorities in mind. In November 2007, Hurricane Noel struck the Dominican Republic, causing the deaths of 85 people and the displacement of tens of thousands. The government had failed to warn residents about the oncoming storm and to anticipate its severity. Meanwhile, the government was criticised for spending too much on ambitious public works, such as the new Metro in the capital city.[104]

Blocking assistance

A small but significant minority of governments and non-state actors are actively abusive towards civilian populations – either their own or those of occupied territories. In 2007, UN Secretary-General Ban Ki-moon reported that conflict was limiting or preventing humanitarian access to over 18

A porter loads supplies onto an
Oxfam helicopter, bound for the
mountainous northern regions of
Pakistan affected by an
earthquake (2005).

Carlo Heathcote / Oxfam

million people in countries like Iraq, Somalia, Sudan, and Afghanistan either due to general insecurity or deliberate obstruction.[105] In 2007, Oxfam was forced to withdraw from Gereida, in Darfur, where it was providing water, sanitation, and health-education services to 130,000 vulnerable people. The withdrawal was brought about by the failure of the local authorities to take steps to improve security, following serious attacks on humanitarian workers.

Following the Hamas takeover of the Gaza Strip in June 2007, the Israeli government began a blockade of the territory, severely restricting supplies of fuel, food, medical equipment, and other items. In November 2008, Israel intensified its 18-month blockade of the Gaza Strip forcing UNRWA to temporarily suspend food aid distribution to 750,000 people, halting a cash for work programme for 94,000 people and leaving half the population in Gaza City with piped water only once a week for a few hours.[106] But this was only one of the most severe examples of the ongoing consequences of the blockade for the civilian population in Gaza, the effects of which constituted collective punishment of ordinary men, women, and children – an act illegal under international law.[107]

Where civilians are actively targeted in conflict, talking about state–citizen accountability is largely an irrelevance. In these situations, two things are required: first, impartial international humanitarian assistance, aimed at saving lives and preserving livelihoods in the immediate term; second, courageous international action to challenge states' behaviour.

International humanitarian assistance

In 2007, more than 40 million people around the world benefited from humanitarian assistance provided under UN appeals.[108] Millions more benefit from humanitarian aid provided outside these appeals. At its best, international humanitarian assistance works alongside national structures to provide timely and appropriate assistance that complements and reinforces the state's capacity.

At its worst, assistance is too little, too late, sometimes inappropriate and sub-standard. International humanitarian assistance has been improving, but it is still tragically inconsistent. How can it improve further so that everyone in need gets the assistance they deserve from both local and international providers? The next chapter addresses that question.

A woman fills a water container with clean water supplied from an Oxfam-installed water system, northern Pakistan, 2005. Oxfam humanitarian staff work according to SPHERE minimum standards in disaster response, which includes ensuring key indicators are met for the provision of safe water for drinking, cooking, and personal and domestic hygiene needs (www.sphereproject.org).

Dan Chung / Guardian Newspapers Ltd

4

Quality, impartiality and accountability in international humanitarian aid

Dedi was one of 1,800 inhabitants out of an original 10,000 to survive the destruction of Leupung in Aceh, Indonesia, when the Indian Ocean tsunami struck in December 2004. For him and his community, humanitarian assistance was important not only for establishing a means of survival, but for re-establishing a degree of normality, dignity, and control over their lives:

> We knew we needed a lot of assistance, either from the government, or from other countries through the NGOs...We knew Leupung needed help, so we decided to go and find someone...to help us. We heard about Oxfam from the Red Cross, so we went to their office in Banda Aceh.[109]

International humanitarian assistance can be vital to people like Dedi. First, international agencies can help build, reinforce, or complement domestic capacity to respond in crises. Second, they can provide assistance directly in situations where conflict, political negligence, or simply a lack of resources make domestic assistance out of the question. This is the ideal, but it is all too often an elusive one. Too much of the assistance delivered by international relief agencies is poor quality, poorly co-ordinated, and unaccountable; some is even provided in a way that is harmful. Too many aid resources are allocated partially, according to political or security priorities, or in response to media coverage. Many international responses pay scant regard to working with national governments or with local civil society.

For Oxfam, five issues are key to improving the delivery of humanitarian assistance so that it is fit for purpose in the twenty-first century. People affected by emergencies deserve aid that is more than just an empty gesture of support. They deserve aid that:

'I had to flee my village because of attacks by the military. If I hadn't managed to reach this camp we would have died,' Karo and her baby, Happiness, Bulengo camp, Goma, Democratic Republic of Congo (2008).

Suzi O'Keefe / Oxfam

1 saves lives (that is relevant, good quality, and well-managed);
2 is delivered impartially on the basis of need;
3 is accountable, with mechanisms to challenge failure and abuse;
4 builds durable solutions; and
5 is sufficiently resourced.

In this chapter, we will look at how humanitarian assistance can best meet the first three objectives. The last two are addressed in Chapters 5 and 6 respectively.

Aid that saves lives

Relevance and quality

Humanitarian assistance should be of sufficient quality to allow people to survive emergencies, addressing their basic need for food, clean water, sanitation, shelter, and medical assistance. Poor-quality aid can damage people's prospects of survival. Insufficient food rations, for instance, can affect the nutritional health of vulnerable individuals, while encouraging households to stay put that would otherwise go in search of better prospects.

To help ensure quality assistance, many international humanitarian agencies now have transparent standards for their response: to guide their own work and to advocate to others. The Sphere Humanitarian Charter and Minimum Standards in Disaster Response, originally designed in the late 1990s and revised in 2004, provide a set of minimum requirements for humanitarian response, covering every key aspect including water supply and sanitation, food and nutrition, and shelter. Humanitarian organisations, both local and international, use Sphere and other standards to lobby local governments, donors, and other aid providers to facilitate better aid.[110] It is not unknown for affected communities themselves to use Sphere minimum standards to hold Oxfam staff to account.[111]

But international humanitarian agencies have not always been consistent in the application of standards, and the quality of many humanitarian programmes still falls well below the standard recipients have the right to expect. The following sections look at two areas that must improve: targeting the most vulnerable people, and co-ordinating the total effort.

Food scarcity

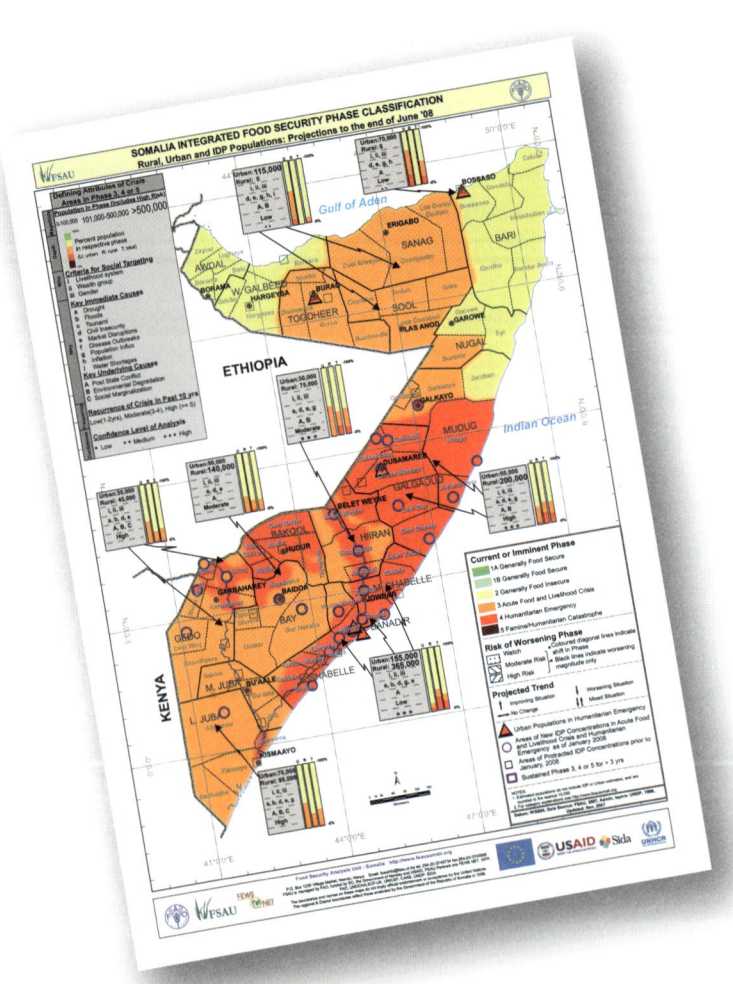

This map shows an innovative method to assess and present areas of food insecurity. The Integrated Food Security Phase Classification (IPC) was originally developed in the context of Somalia in 2004 by the Food Security Analysis Unit (FSAU)/FAO Somalia.

When the Somali state collapsed in the early 1990s, FSAU was created to provide overall food security analysis, as well as key information on livelihoods, crop production, market prices, nutrition, and others.

Effective targeting

The adequate assessment of the needs of affected populations is one area where past humanitarian responses have suffered from endemic weakness.[112] Effectively assessing needs, with the participation of the affected community, is crucial to help decide on the best way to help people, to find the most appropriate partners, and to work out which emergencies should be given priority for resources. Analysing the most vulnerable groups in any given population is vital in order to understand who is most affected by an emergency, what they require, and what capacity they have to help themselves. Vulnerability will be defined by gender, age, physical health, and ethnicity, among other factors. Yet too many assessments still ignore these vulnerabilities based on identity, treating the affected population as essentially undifferentiated, and responding accordingly. This is not because humanitarian agencies lack the knowledge to do this, but because they fail to treat it as a priority.

Giving needs assessment the priority it deserves is vital, but two other things must also be done. The first is providing sufficient and flexible funding to make those speedy and effective assessments possible. International donors have not done all they should to make sure that dedicated funding is available; indeed many donors refuse to fund such assessments.

The second is being better prepared. If local government, civil society – even international humanitarian organisations – do not already have in place the skills, resources, or agreed methodology to conduct needs assessment, valuable time is often lost when emergencies occur and there is a scramble to get organised. Preparedness to carry out assessment should be seen as fundamental to overall emergency preparedness.

With better assessments, there can be no excuse for failure to target those most vulnerable in humanitarian crises. Any response should be sensitive to the specific needs that arise from gender, age, ethnic group, and so on, and respond to what particular groups need and ask for. Despite much rhetoric, many aid programmes still fall short of this. Some unwittingly exacerbate existing inequalities, such as those between women and men, or, sometimes despite the best intentions, they place beneficiaries at risk of violence. In Goz Amir camp in Chad, women played a pivotal role in assessing and implementing Oxfam's public-health activities. They were given a rare opportunity to obtain paid employment and learn marketable new skills. In doing this, there was a danger of creating potential resentment from men

A boat jointly operated by Oxfam and MSF, Freetown, Sierra Leone (2001).

Crispin Hughes / Oxfam

and community leaders, who might see women encroaching on traditionally male roles and benefiting disproportionately from aid. It was important to ensure that women worked alongside male beneficiaries and community leaders, and that this work was seen as beneficial to both women and men. [113]

Good co-ordination and leadership

Since the African Great Lakes crisis of the mid-1990s, the world has seen a significant increase in the number of operational humanitarian agencies and donors. On the one hand, this growth means more skills and capacity. On the other, it means that there is more competition for resources and media attention, and potentially more confusion in co-ordination among all the different agencies on the ground. [114] The weak initial humanitarian response to the Darfur crisis, for instance, was attributed in great part to poor co-ordination.

The consequences of poor co-ordination can be significant. Whole communities may miss out on assistance, while others receive more aid than they need. Areas like food and public health may be covered by several agencies, while other needs, such as protecting beneficiaries from violence, may be ignored. [115] Bad co-ordination also undermines states' accountability; it is almost impossible for states to take responsibility for an emergency response when the division of labour between government, the UN, and humanitarian agencies is not clear.

In 2005, the UN commissioned the *Humanitarian Response Review*, partly in response to such concerns. [116] This recommended a number of improvements to co-ordination and funding, including the so-called 'cluster approach', which gave different UN agencies responsibility for particular 'sectors' (water, sanitation and hygiene, food, etc.). In specific countries, different UN agencies have led 'clusters' at the national level too. A 2007 evaluation found that the cluster approach had resulted in some systemic improvement in overall humanitarian response and leadership. [117] But it had also generally suffered from poor engagement with national governments, despite exceptions, such as the Philippines where the government co-ordinates the clusters. And there are no effective means to challenge poor performance in real time either at field or at global level. UN agencies have been slow to prioritise their 'cluster lead' responsibilities, with insufficient resources trickling down to each country. Partnerships between UN agencies and international NGOs have

UN Emergency Relief
Coordinator John Holmes visits
displaced people in conflict-hit
Molo, Rift Valley Province, Kenya,
February 2008.

improved slowly, but local civil society has not been sufficiently engaged. Concerns have also been voiced about whether the cluster system would be effective if faced with multiple, simultaneous emergencies.[118]

The importance of leadership

The UN can play a key role in providing leadership in humanitarian crises. But the persistent failure to recruit competent and experienced UN Humanitarian Coordinators (HCs – the officials employed by the UN to oversee humanitarian response in a given country) has been widely recognised by people inside and outside the UN.[119] In 2008, a British development minister, Gareth Thomas, criticised the UN's lack of progress, saying that this 'lack of leadership costs lives'.[120]

The establishment of an office within OCHA dedicated to improving recruitment and training of potential HCs will go some way towards expanding and diversifying the pool of HCs, and providing them with training and support.[121] But the problems go much deeper than just training – or even necessarily recruitment procedures. The role of HC is absolutely key to effective international humanitarian response worldwide, but efforts to improve their recruitment and performance have not been given nearly high enough priority among other humanitarian reforms.[122] Furthermore, the combining of the HC role with other key UN roles ('double-hatting' or even 'triple-hatting' with roles like each country's UN Resident Coordinator or the Deputy Special Representative of the Secretary-General) dilutes HCs' ability to function effectively, and generates conflicts of interest. It is unrealistic to expect one person adequately to fulfil all these roles. And, as we examine in the next section, it is unacceptable not to have a 'fire-wall' between humanitarian activities on the one hand, and the UN's political and military functions on the other.

Aid that is impartial

Impartiality is not just an abstract principle. It is understood and valued by many of those who receive humanitarian aid.[123] In the aftermath of floods in Indonesia in 2007, Oxfam implemented a cash-for-work programme. It was a time of high political tension in the run-up to an election, so it was particularly important that cash was clearly distributed impartially and accountably. Budiono, from Bina Swagiri, Oxfam's partner organisation, explained that impartiality, like justice, has to be seen to be done:

'We were very happy because everyone knew what was to happen.' Sri Haryani, who received cash as part of a programme implemented by Oxfam and its partner Bina Swagiri, Indonesia (2008).

Jane Beesley / Oxfam GB

[The community] say, 'This is like aid from the angels' – it's untouched...there's no corruption... There are no suspicions on any level or concerns that there will be corruption over the cash, and the community hope that programmes from the government will also be like this.[124]

It was made clear that the money was coming from Oxfam and Bina Swagiri, and people were told that the money was being given only on the basis of need. Sri Haryani, a local resident and cash recipient, explained: 'We've all read the notice [a signed agreement between the partner and Oxfam]; it's pinned up where we can all read it...It was in the open in front of everyone.'[125]

Receiving aid on the basis of need – and in a way that is not dictated by political, military, or any other interests – is vital for two main reasons. First, and most obviously, it allows aid to be channelled to those who need it most. Second, it reduces the likelihood of aid creating resentment and accusations of bias, and from that the potential for threats both to the humanitarian operation itself, and sometimes to the lives of those involved. If aid is seen to be impartial, it reduces the possibility that either *receiving* or *providing* aid is perceived as political, with consequent dangers.

In Colombia, for example, some communities have refused desperately needed relief from the government for fear of violent reprisals from armed groups. In Afghanistan and many other crises, aid workers have been targeted because insurgents have seen them as tools of an international intervention. According to a 2008 study in Iraq, the perceived link between humanitarian agencies and the multinational force has severely curtailed the ability of humanitarian agencies to operate.[126] This reflects a wider global trend: an unprecedented growth in violent attacks on the staff of humanitarian organisations, with an increasing proportion of attacks specifically directed at aid workers for political reasons, rather than random violence or robbery.[127] Belligerents in many conflicts see it as in their interest to target and kill civilians and those who try to help them.[128] The best efforts of humanitarian agencies to demonstrate impartiality may not always be enough to prevent this.

Much has been written, particularly since the onset of the 'war on terror', about governments recruiting humanitarian agencies into their overall political and military strategies – to be, as Colin Powell once put it, 'force multipliers' in the counter-terrorist effort. Much of that criticism has been entirely valid, and governments have still not learnt the lessons from it. However, international humanitarian organisations themselves have

Pakistani troops unload relief
supplies for earthquake victims
from a US Chinook helicopter,
Muzaffarabad, Pakistan (2005).

Edward Parsons / IRIN

too often failed to do enough to ensure that they are perceived as impartial in conflict. According to one major US NGO, the use of both coalition forces and private contractors to provide relief aid in the wake of the US-led invasion of Iraq '... blurred the distinction between humanitarian agencies, contractors and military actors'.[129] Yet, in 2007, other major NGOs still maintained very close relationships with coalition forces in Iraq, using both coalition military and private contractors to provide security for their humanitarian operations.[130]

The UN too has blurred the distinction between its political and military role and its humanitarian activities by combining these functions under unified management in so called 'integrated missions'. In Afghanistan, the continued refusal of the UN to create a 'fire-wall' between its humanitarian and military functions has done nothing to undermine insurgents' perception that the whole UN mission is working for, in their eyes, a hostile Western invasion. In just the first seven months of 2008, some 30 aid workers in Afghanistan were killed in insurgent attacks.[131]

Governments, some NGOs, the UN, and others must all learn to maintain a clear distinction between, on the one hand, civilian humanitarian and, on the other, military actors. While in crises like Afghanistan, governments obviously seek to bring all the tools at their disposal to bear to secure their objectives, they must not do so at the cost of humanitarian agencies' independence and, more importantly, civilians' need to receive aid impartially. Good communication between civil and military agencies involved in each crisis should not mean that aid primarily serves political or security purposes – rather than saving lives or reducing poverty.

None of this should suggest, however, that the provision of assistance by military forces is wrong *per se*. In some countries – notably, throughout South, East, and South-East Asia – national armies play a key role in delivering relief, as well as moving people in advance of disasters and in disaster recovery. When an earthquake struck Pakistan and India in October 2005, military forces from Australia, Libya, the United Arab Emirates, and Afghanistan as well as staff from the UN, NATO, and private humanitarian organisations, such as MSF and Oxfam, joined the Pakistan military in providing the airlift capacity required to get assistance to those in need.

In conflict, warring parties have a legal obligation to facilitate humanitarian aid to civilian populations. But there are real risks attached to the use of military forces to distribute relief in conflict. Ultimately, if humanitarian assistance is perceived as coming from one or other

Members of the Indian battalion of the United Nations Organization Mission in the Democratic Republic of Congo (MONUC), Goma, DRC (2008).

Marie Frechon / UN

belligerent party, more aid workers may be killed – and men, women, and children may not get the life-saving assistance that they urgently need. Various international guidelines exist on the use of military assets in relief response, and they must be followed.[132] In conflict, the basic rule must be that military assets should only be used to distribute relief when no civilian alternative is available.[133]

Dialogue between humanitarian agencies and military policy makers is essential to overcome the misunderstandings that still exist between them. While humanitarian agencies have engaged actively with many NATO governments, there is also an urgent need to engage with the key contributors to multilateral peacekeeping operations – Nigeria, Pakistan, India, Bangladesh – to ensure that best practice is followed. [134]

Humanitarian assistance and conflict sensitivity

Humanitarian assistance is often provided in situations where conflict is an everyday fact of life. Those to whom aid is provided may be aligned (or perceived to be aligned) to particular political or military interests. In other circumstances, security may be so poor that aid itself presents a security risk to recipients. For three months in 2007, families in Kisharo, in the DRC, who were in obvious need of assistance, told international NGOs to stop distributing plastic sheeting, as they feared being attacked by looters more than they feared being without shelter.[135] In such circumstances, the challenge for humanitarian agencies is to avoid placing at risk those with whom they work, and to identify how programmes can support the reduction of communities' vulnerability to conflict.[136]

Yet few providers of humanitarian assistance employ the skills needed to assess the risks of exacerbating conflict in their programmes, even though donors have begun to require them to include conflict-sensitivity planning in much of their work.[137] The initial stages of the international humanitarian response in Darfur were criticised for failing to take account of the underlying causes of that conflict.[138] Conflict impact assessments are frequently neglected in favour of immediate life-saving activities.

Humanitarian programming often takes place in volatile settings, where staff turnover is high, analytical capacity is weak, and lessons are not always learned. The moral, political, and financial pressures to respond, and to be seen to respond, emphasise acting over thinking.[139] Building conflict sensitivity in humanitarian organisations requires a long-term approach to developing skills as well as solid, and ongoing, conflict

Cash being distributed as part of
an Oxfam cash-for-work
programme in Indonesia. The
cash is counted out in front of the
beneficiaries in a public meeting
(2008).

Jane Beesley / Oxfam GB

assessment on the ground, both prior to and during humanitarian programmes. Assessments should be based on strong, transparent, and accountable links with local communities.[140] Working with local organisations can also help to improve analysis of local conflict dynamics, and to ensure that programme design and activities are sensitive to their potential impact on conflict.

Aid that is accountable

Before...there was no one to listen to us. With encouragement [from SEED, one of Oxfam's partners] we went to town by bus to visit the Kachcheri [local government agent]...he was really shocked. We told him we had no transport for emergencies and he gave us a trishaw, which we still use. We asked [him] for a hut for shade and he gave it to us. The shopkeepers always give us less dry rations than they're supposed to. We asked the government agent for a set of scales so we can check the weights.[141]

Discussion with a women's group, Sithamparapuram camp, Sri Lanka

Unless women and men can hold their government (or any other provider) to account for the assistance that they should get, that assistance is unlikely to be adequate, appropriate, or equitable. Unfortunately, emergencies tend to weaken the accountability between the state and its citizens. Disasters often disrupt or destroy communications, render basic-service infrastructure useless, and stop government agencies functioning. Catastrophic events may destroy or displace communities, making people less confident about making demands of government agencies. And, as we have already seen, those states in which people are most vulnerable to emergencies are often those where the bonds of accountability between state and citizen are weakest to start with.

In many emergencies, international assistance may further complicate matters. In providing assistance, aid organisations risk absolving governments of their obligations and reducing the likelihood of basic services being restored. International humanitarian agencies themselves have little direct accountability to those they work with. Although recent efforts have been made by some agencies to address this, most still have a very long way to go before they have fulfilled their own standards.

How then can people be empowered in emergencies to exercise control over the humanitarian aid directed to them, and to hold those engaged in its provision accountable? What can international agencies do to help?

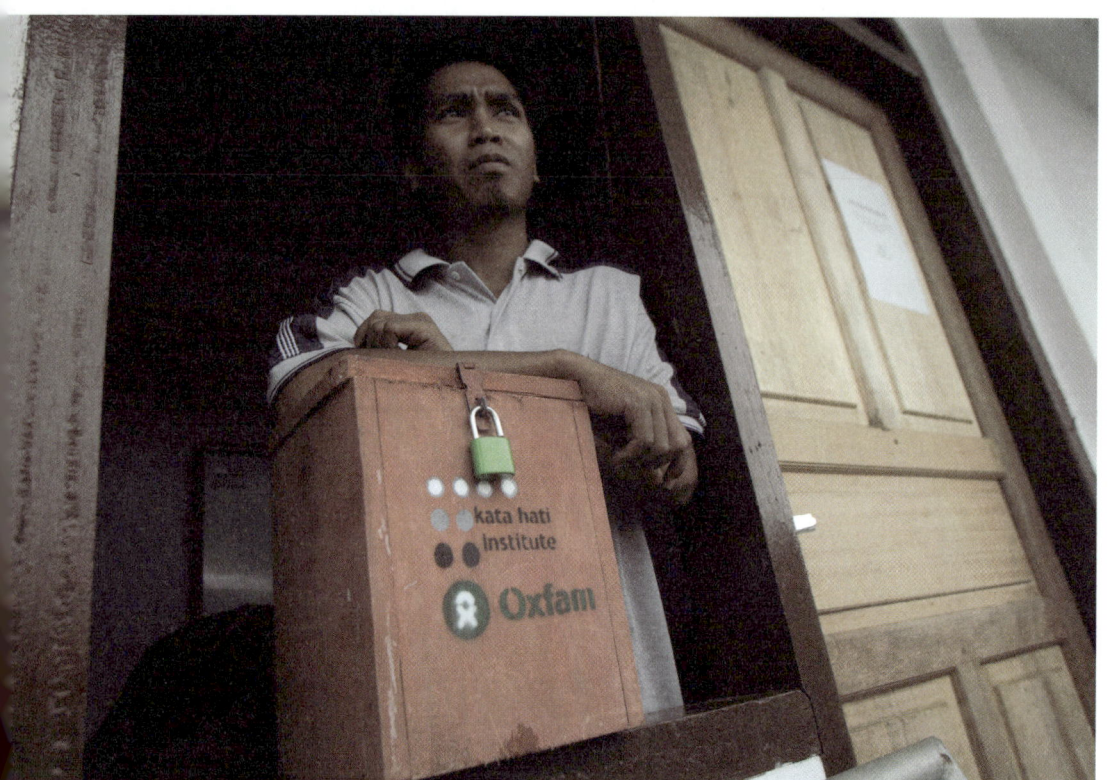

M Yaqob, of Kata Hati Institute, Indonesia, installs a lockable box for the organisation's beneficiaries to give suggestions and make complaints. Kata Hati Institute is funded by Oxfam for this project (2005).

Jim Holmes / Oxfam GB

If humanitarian assistance is to be responsive, it needs to be transparent and to promote participation by aid recipients. Its decision-making processes should be open and well communicated. During the 2006 food crisis in Malawi, affected communities selected the people eligible for Oxfam's programme in a public forum, using mutually agreed criteria. Representatives – both women and men – from the affected communities were integral to deciding how a complaints mechanism should be set up. In a sample of 1,100 people interviewed in a subsequent evaluation, all said that they knew the rations that they were entitled to, how to collect this entitlement, and who was responsible for delivering them. They were also aware of their rights, knowing, for example, that they did not need to give anything in return for what was provided, as well as how to seek redress if this was demanded.

Organisational and financial transparency is needed too; publishing (where local security conditions allow) contact details, budgets, and project plans in places where aid recipients can get access to them.[142] Oxfam uses public-information boards in many of its project sites, and public meetings or other media such as leaflets or local newspapers.

Perhaps more importantly still, humanitarian agencies must have clear mechanisms to allow aid recipients to complain about failure and abuse. In 2002, a joint UNHCR and Save the Children report highlighted the widespread sexual exploitation and abuse taking place in camps for refugees and internally displaced people in West Africa, perpetrated by the very people there to protect them: national and international NGO staff, UN staff, and peacekeeping troops.[143] This and subsequent revelations have demonstrated that no agency can be complacent about the risk of sexual abuse and exploitation by their staff. In Zimbabwe, Oxfam worked specifically to prevent sexual exploitation and abuse by staff and partners involved in providing food to displaced people. Oxfam staff and partners, alongside the elected Village Distribution Committees and others, selected those to receive the aid in a transparent forum that allowed them to clearly and fairly identify those most in need. Oxfam explained the distribution process to the people affected by the emergency, as well as letting them know about their entitlement to assistance (explaining that they need not provide sex, or anything else, in exchange for their ration).[144] Suggestion boxes provided an anonymous way for people to raise issues and concerns. Although initially there was reluctance from Oxfam's partner – based on suspicions that boxes were initially tampered with – the idea took hold, and was taken up by the partner outside of Oxfam programmes.[145]

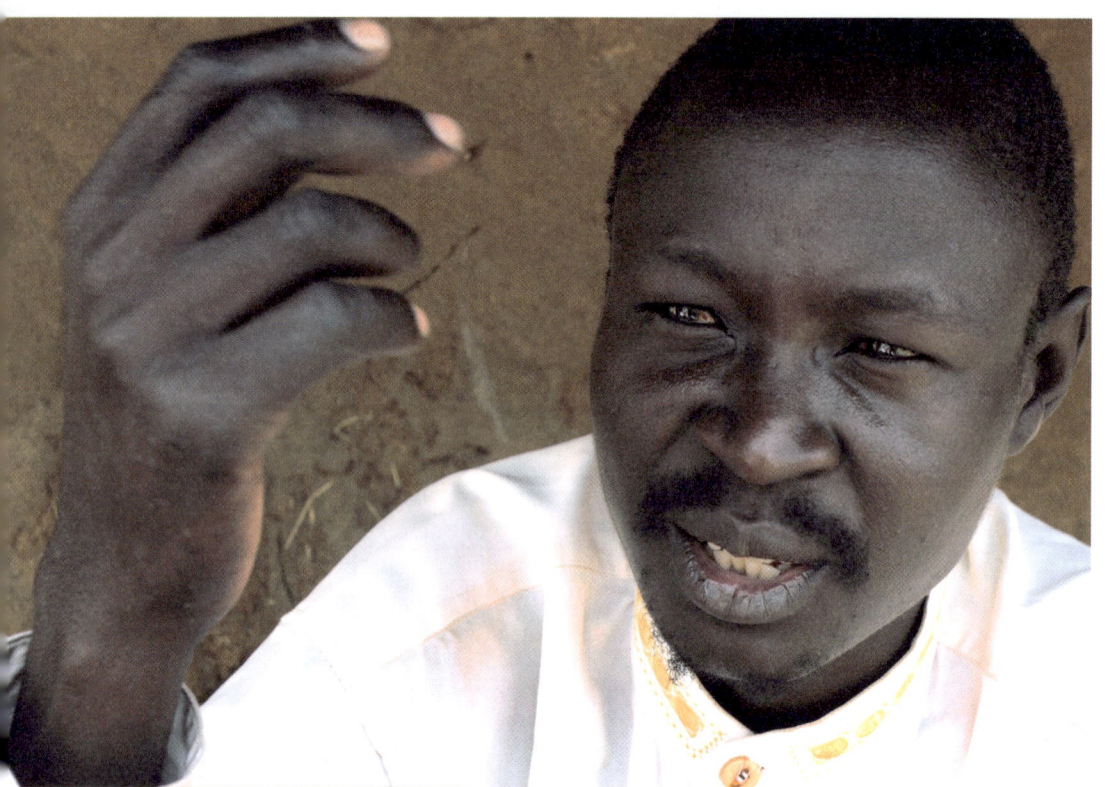

Geoff Sayer / Oxfam GB

'To me, the method Oxfam used was good. Oxfam gave responsibility to community leaders.' Simon Opedun, whose role as a 'community resource person' was partly to diagnose and refer health problems, partly to represent his community's needs to local government authorities. (Uganda, 2007)

At the same time, international providers of humanitarian assistance have a duty to ensure that, wherever possible, they invest in local human and material capacity. This is hardly a new concept,[146] yet some international humanitarian agencies and aid workers continue to argue that it slows down response. This ignores the fact that local civil society and local government are often best placed to respond effectively on the ground. Critically, failing to work through local bodies reduces the likelihood that sustainable structures will be established to deal with the effects of future crises. In parts of northern Uganda, Oxfam has worked through local village councils and district authorities to carry out relief activities. This was in part because, prior to the 2006 'cessation of hostilities' between the government and the Lord's Resistance Army, poor security often prevented Oxfam from implementing its own activities in the region.[147] But this way of working also has the practical advantages of, first, helping to build sustainable local services; and second, reinforcing the accountability of local authorities. This decentralised way of working has had a significant impact on reducing aid dependency in a context of chronic humanitarian need. At the same time, Oxfam's emphasis on principles of quality and rights to assistance has boosted the community's ability and will to demand better services for themselves from their government.

Looking to the long term

Many international humanitarian organisations, at least in theory, recognise the need to involve people affected by emergencies in project assessment, design, and monitoring. Many have now implemented complaints mechanisms for specific projects. This is right, and a vital way to make humanitarian interventions more relevant, focused, and sustainable – and to meet the standards for effective aid that most agencies have set themselves.

This chapter has looked at a number of issues concerning how to improve the quality of immediate humanitarian response. That is, however, only part of what needs to be done. Addressing long-term vulnerability to disasters will also require international humanitarian organisations to expand their repertoire of work. They must look beyond those traditional humanitarian aid interventions that address immediate threats to life. Saving life is, of course, the priority, but in most contexts, there is no reason why acting to save lives should preclude reducing vulnerability to future emergencies as well. In Chapter 5, we look at some of the strategies that can be employed to achieve this.

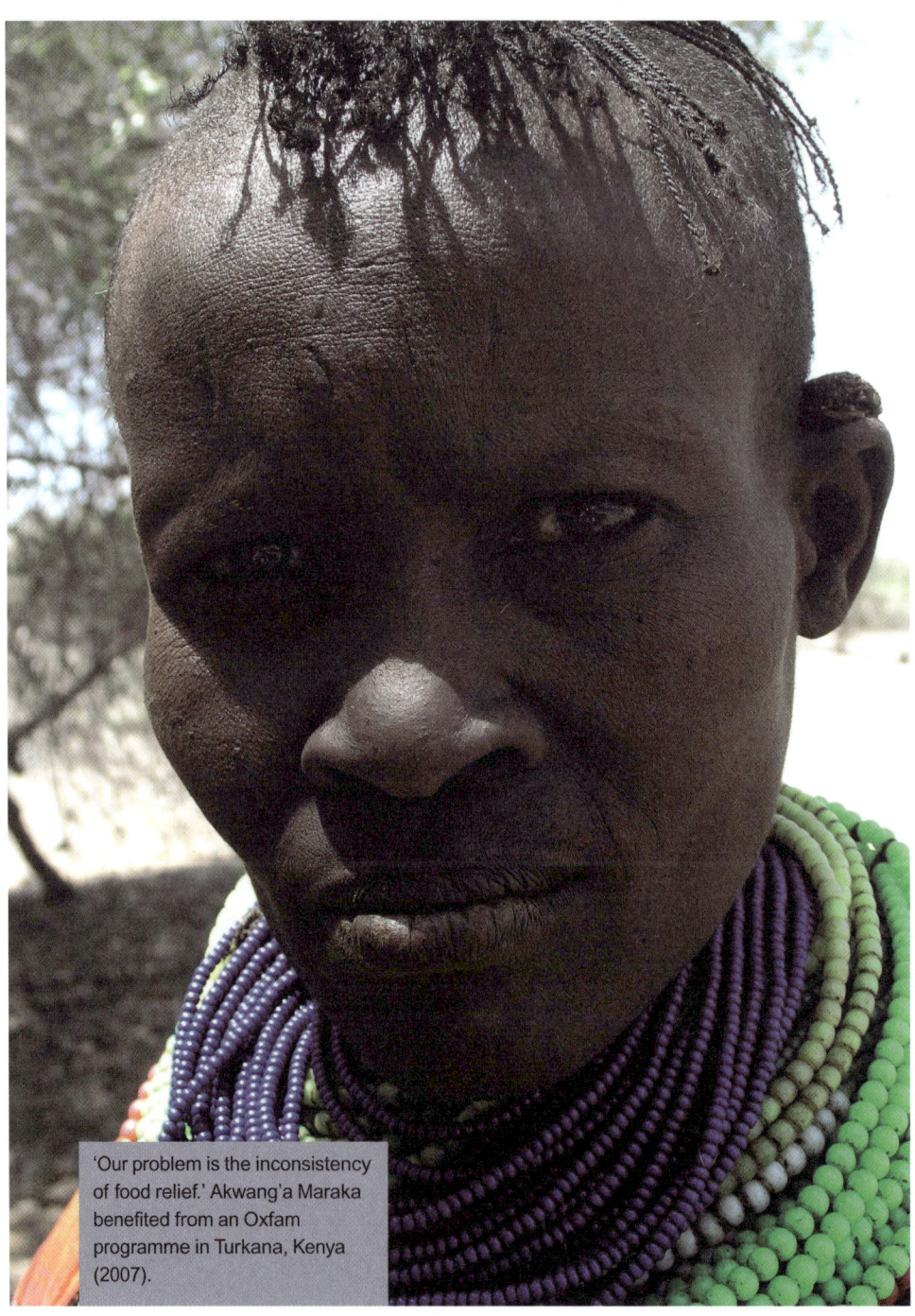

'Our problem is the inconsistency of food relief.' Akwang'a Maraka benefited from an Oxfam programme in Turkana, Kenya (2007).

Jane Beesley / Oxfam GB

5

Long-term solutions to long-term problems

Now food relief is coming to an end and you can see that we are still struggling...So even what we have started, like these small businesses, once food relief stops, we'll end up using what we've acquired or bought [to feed ourselves].

Akwang'a Maraka, Turkana, Kenya, 2007[148]

For Akwang'a and her neighbour, Anna Pedo, food is scarce every year, threatening both her own life and those of her family. This happens regardless of whether the world declares an emergency. 'We have received food relief in the past, but it's not reliable', explains Anna. 'Sometimes we get, sometimes we don't get...And when relief ends, we are left with nothing.'[149] Akwang'a's experience is by no means unique. Those who manage and deliver humanitarian aid often get caught up in arguments about what constitutes an emergency, when an emergency begins or ends, or whether needs are chronic and require more long-term development solutions. But, from the perspective of those in need of assistance, such definitions make little sense. People like Akwang'a and Anna require timely emergency assistance when their lives are threatened by lack of food. But they also need the world to recognise that such food scarcity is for them a persistent and debilitating threat – one which can be mitigated or even removed if only aid organisations and governments take a longer-term view.

'Humanitarian' versus 'development'?

A former UN High Commissioner for Refugees, Sadako Ogata, once famously stated that 'there are no humanitarian solutions for humanitarian problems'.[150] True, the root causes of humanitarian problems – authoritarian government, unfair land distribution, ethnic discrimination, resource conflicts – require more fundamental solutions than humanitarian programmes or agencies can offer. But relief work can and should work to reduce vulnerability in the longer term. The imperative to save lives sometimes demands interventions such as the provision of drinking water in refugee camps or the provision of in-kind

Sidadhaya Moidi clearing weed from a millet field in Borem District, Mali. The effects of desertification, erratic rainfall, frequent locust invasions, and lack of access to equitable markets make Borem highly vulnerable to food scarcity (2005).

Dave Clark / Oxfam

food aid. But these short-term strategies are not the only tools available to relief workers; humanitarian projects should contribute to tackling the different factors that make people vulnerable to disasters. The traditional distinctions between 'emergency' intervention, reconstruction, and longer-term approaches to vulnerability do not help this to happen. In this chapter, we look at how long-term needs can be addressed in response to risks like food scarcity, storms and floods and how breaking down some of the barriers between 'humanitarian' and 'development' can help.

Food scarcity

Nearly 3 million Africans die of hunger-related causes every year – almost six people per minute – and one in every three Africans is undernourished.[151] Neither is Africa by any means the only continent affected by food insecurity – the inability of households to obtain sufficient food. Half the world's underweight children live in South Asia.[152] Globally, the number of food crises has doubled over the past two decades to more than 30 per year since the turn of the millennium.[153]

But the language of crisis is often misleading. Most food crises are far more deeply rooted than is suggested by the idea of a famine: a time-bound event that arrives, is dealt with, and goes away. In many parts of Ethiopia, levels of child malnutrition and mortality figures regularly exceed what would constitute an emergency in other parts of the world. This is replicated across Africa's arid Sahel region. In Niger, each year and irrespective of harvest, drought, or food prices, children are malnourished and die in numbers that are far beyond those that would normally trigger emergency response.[154] The culprit is not a single, catastrophic famine, but decades of chronic poverty – permanent, insidious, deadly. The erosion of agricultural subsistence livelihoods, the increase of communicable disease including HIV and AIDS, poor water quality, and poor sanitation are common factors underpinning the majority of food emergencies. Food crises arise, not merely from natural causes, but from poverty and injustice that bar access to productive land, water, and affordable credit, and from the degradation of natural resources. Climate change, along with the enforced liberalisation of markets, is already compounding this grim picture.

Jim Holmes / Oxfam GB

A road under construction as part of a cash-for-work programme, Rundeng, Indonesia. Unlike food distributions, providing cash for work supports local food production, and cash recipients can also save the money they receive in order to invest in income generation, education or housing (2005).

In-kind food aid

For decades, the world's response to food 'crises' has been to provide food itself directly at the point of need: in-kind food aid. Sometimes it is necessary to do this to save lives, particularly where war or natural disaster has interrupted food production and supply. In Darfur in 2008, the World Food Program (WFP) and its partners distributed more than 20,000 tons of food every month to more than 2 million people scattered over an area the size of France. Such in-kind food aid still represents the bulk of international relief.[155]

But distributing food itself, as opposed to other types of aid, can have significant disadvantages. Particularly when it is imported in bulk from outside an affected region, it can undermine local food production and markets, and so make people more vulnerable in future.[156] Purchasing food locally avoids this, and recognising this, in 2008 WFP launched the Purchase for Progress initiative, which will see 350,000 smallholders in the developing world benefit from contracts to provide food to UN programmes.[157]

Alternatives

There is a wide range of alternatives to distributing food itself, many of which offer more sustainable solutions to underlying food insecurity. Giving people 'cash for work' can help to protect fragile local food markets in emergencies, particularly when cash contributions are 'index linked' to changes in food prices. In Viet Nam, Oxfam implemented a cash-for-work programme in Nam Dinh Province after Typhoon Damrey. The typhoon had caused extensive damage, but food was still being produced and local markets were still functioning. The provision of cash allowed poor households to meet their needs with items available locally, while local producers also benefited. At the same time, Oxfam distributed grants to help start rebuilding local businesses and farms.

Cash for work is not a panacea, however, and other alternatives may be much more appropriate in certain contexts. In pastoralist areas, droughts may cause livestock to die in large numbers, and pastoral communities may find it impossible to sell their livestock for cash to buy food because local markets may have collapsed. The best option may be for governments or others to buy livestock at a fair price before the crisis intensifies, giving pastoralists some income and reducing the number of animals competing

Beneficiaries of the Ethiopian government's Productive Safety Net programme. Because of their age, they receive direct support and do not have to take part in public works activities. They receive a monthly cash or food transfer equivalent to half a monthly food ration, for six months of the year (Oromiya, Ethiopia, 2008).

for scarce water and fodder. This is particularly important for pastoralists who depend on the survival of their livestock – meat, milk, and other animal products are difficult to stockpile, unlike horticultural produce. As elsewhere, it is early intervention that is vital to stop chronic vulnerability turning into acute need, which costs vastly more to address.[158]

From technical advice and support to help affected people find new livelihoods, to projects to build or repair transport infrastructure, alternatives to food aid abound. What is required is the vision to identify the most appropriate responses and sufficient reliable and flexible resources to implement them.

Government action and social protection

Three-quarters of the world's poor people live in rural areas, most of them on small farms. It is now widely recognised that adequate investment in agriculture, and especially support to smallholders, is the only way to reduce their hunger and vulnerability.

The scale of the challenge far outweighs the amount of money currently available, however. In 2007, the amount of development aid allocated to agriculture was only about $4bn – compared with the estimated $125bn in direct payments to farmers in OECD countries in 2006. Meanwhile, developing-country governments are failing to invest sufficiently in agriculture. In 2005, only six out of 24 African governments had met their 2003 commitment to spend 10 per cent of their budgets on agriculture. If all African governments were to meet that target, an extra $5bn would be raised.[159]

Once again, national governments bear primary responsibility for addressing vulnerability to food scarcity. They can and must do so, both by investing in agriculture and by providing targeted benefits (social protection measures) to vulnerable people. In Brazil, since the 1990s, a comprehensive programme of support to poor farming households has reduced the prevalence of malnutrition from 10 per cent in 1999 to 2.4 per cent in 2006. Child mortality has reduced by a staggering 45 per cent in the same period.

Other countries are following suit. In Ethiopia, the Productive Safety Net Programme (PSNP) provides benefits (for the most part, in cash) to many of Ethiopia's 7.2 million people who are chronically vulnerable to food scarcity. Critically, vulnerable people receive this help whether the harvest

David Vinuales/Oxfam GB

A child leans against a flood meter, northeastern Nicaragua. Oxfam is working with partners to help communities living along the Bocay and Coco rivers to install an early warning system. The system allows communities to identify when there is a danger of flooding and take appropriate action.

is good or bad, thus enabling poor families to build up assets and to invest in household livelihoods, health, and education. Families with members who are able to work are given benefits in return for participating in public works; those who cannot (elderly or ill people) are given benefits directly. A 2006 evaluation concluded that the scheme, although not without its challenges, was already having a significant impact on poor households: increasing food availability, reducing asset loss, assisting productive investment (such as education), and enabling people to seek credit to develop their livelihoods.[160]

Reducing the risk from climatic shocks

Following events such as flooding, earthquakes, droughts, and hurricanes, humanitarian assistance focuses on protecting lives from the immediate consequences, including malnutrition, communicable disease, and exposure.

As we explored in Chapter 2, however, the world is experiencing an increase in the frequency and severity of climate-related hazards. People affected by flooding one year are unlikely to escape such threats in the future unless the reasons underlying their vulnerability are addressed; those affected by tropical storms can be more or less certain that they will return in the next hurricane season. In this context, humanitarian *response* is not adequate without preparing for – and seeking to reduce the impact of – the next disaster.

Governments' varied response to risk reduction

At the second World Conference on Disaster Reduction in 2005 in Japan, 168 governments committed to act to take a more sustained and durable approach to reducing the risk from environmental threats. They adopted a ten-year plan, the 'Hyogo Framework for Action', to reduce their citizens' vulnerability to natural hazards.[161] Few governments have lived up to these commitments. Where governments do invest, they often settle for centralised and highly technical projects, like Bangladesh's Flood Action Programme, rather than more local initiatives, which might be better suited to the rising trend of smaller-scale, localised disasters. Indeed Bangladesh, one of the worst disaster-affected countries in the world, has made substantial progress through such local investment, such as cyclone shelters and community-based preparedness systems, evacuation plans,

Jane Beesley / Oxfam

Local residents of Trinidad, Bolivia, cross a bridge between elevated seed-beds, or *camellones*, constructed as part of an Oxfam-supported flood mitigation and food security programme. As Yenny Noza, one of the group working on the *camellones*, pointed out, 'If we have another flood this year, we won't lose all our plants and seeds' (2007).

early warnings, and the mobilisation of volunteers. In 1991 over 138,000 people perished in a cyclone; Bangladesh's subsequent cyclones have killed far fewer people.

The challenge for international humanitarian organisations

Humanitarian organisations have a significant role to play in reducing vulnerability to natural hazards, including by working with government agencies and local civil society. In February 2007, 350,000 people were affected by the worst floods in Bolivia for 40 years. Tens of thousands of hectares of agricultural land were devastated, and some 25,000 people had to be evacuated to temporary shelters.[162] Working with local partners, Oxfam moved quickly to provide water and sanitation and basic hygiene items for 2,000 families. Then, following the return of affected people to their homes, Oxfam set about seeking a more permanent solution. Taking inspiration from a 3,000-year-old pre-Inca agricultural system, Oxfam worked with local municipalities to develop an agricultural system that can cope with regular flooding and drought, improve soil fertility, and make the land productive. The construction of elevated seedbeds, known locally as *camellones*, prevents seasonal floodwater destroying food crops. Around the raised beds are water channels, from which plants are harvested and placed on top of the banks, creating a layer of fertile soil. Because water surrounds the beds, once the system is established there is much less need for watering. Local communities can also supplement their diet with fish, which have re-populated the water channels.[163]

Nevertheless, like many governments, international humanitarian organisations have been slow to support longer-term approaches to disaster preparedness. There are several reasons for this. First, there are the concerns and operational constraints related to mixing humanitarian and development approaches. Second, there are issues about how much it costs. Of course, building community-based preparedness often costs a fraction of a reactive emergency response. In the Dhemaji district of Assam, Oxfam's partner Rural Volunteers Centre has demonstrated that community-based disaster-preparedness costs just 2 per cent of estimated post-flood relief.[164] But for humanitarian organisations – local and international – it is building up organisational capacity in order to implement disaster risk-reduction that is expensive. Staff and training cost money, something that many donors have failed to appreciate.

Jane Beesley / Oxfam

A group of Oxfam-trained youth volunteers from Sandia in Peru, a community particularly vulnerable to landslides caused by seasonal rains. JOVOS (young volunteers for disaster prevention) meet regularly to learn about the risks that Sandia faces and how they can help people to prevent them. They have regular training courses, including first aid and evacuation skills.

Both humanitarian response to emergencies and proactive efforts to reduce vulnerability cost money. Even (or perhaps especially) when the world economy is in decline, governments must invest boldly in emergency-response capacity and reducing the risks associated with disasters. Chapter 6 looks at just how much money is required, where that money should come from, and what systems need to be in place to ensure that it is spent most effectively. The chapter also looks at how new sources of humanitarian action offer greater opportunities to respond more effectively to the changing nature of threats in the twenty-first century.

Will a global recession drive down humanitarian aid budgets?

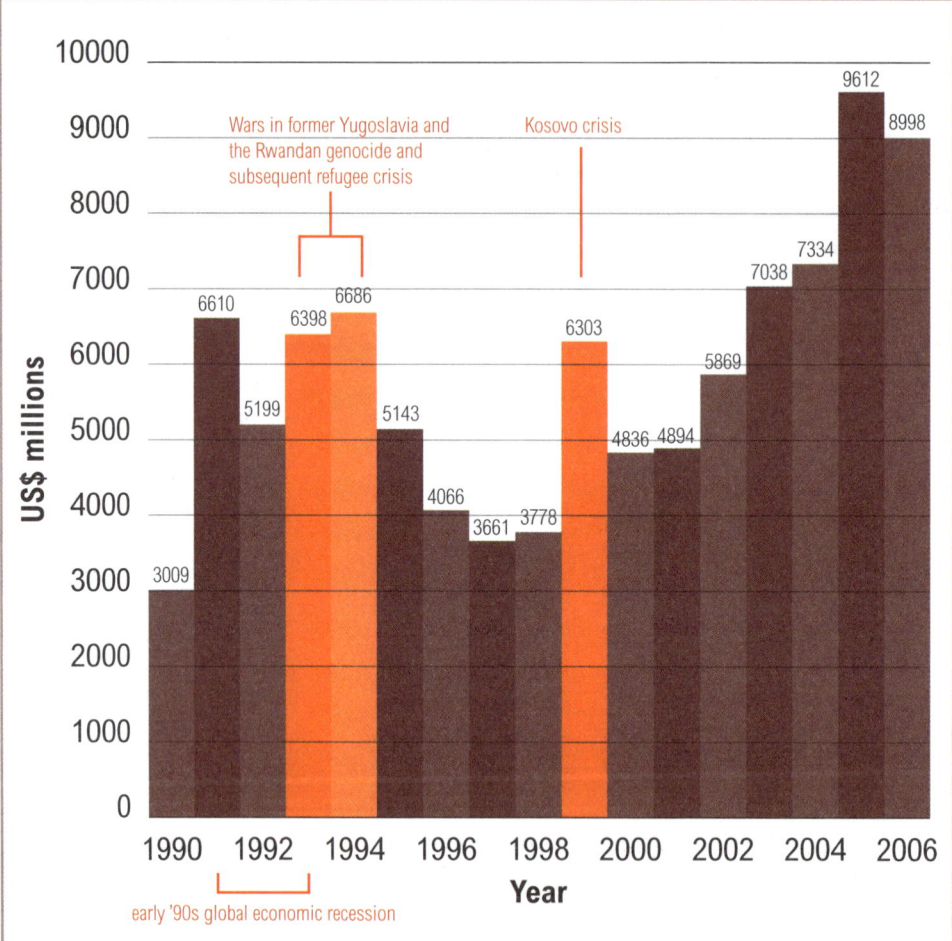

Wars in former Yugoslavia and the Rwandan genocide and subsequent refugee crisis

Kosovo crisis

early '90s global economic recession

US$ millions

Year

3009, 6610, 5199, 6398, 6686, 5143, 4066, 3661, 3778, 6303, 4836, 4894, 5869, 7038, 7334, 9612, 8998

Humanitarian funding from OECD countries has grown for much of the past 10 years. But a longer term analysis of aid trends shows that humanitarian assistance, along with overall overseas development aid, is vulnerable to economic recession. The global economic downturn of 1991-3 saw OECD humanitarian aid budgets fall for a prolonged period. They did not return to a secure upward trend until 2002. While there were two signficant 'spikes' in humanitarian aid during this period – the first in 1993-4, corresponding with the Yugoslav wars and the Rwandan genocide, and the second in response to the Kosovo crisis in 1999 – these were driven by unprecedented public and political interest in the OECD countries. The great majority of emergencies during this period received nothing like the same funding. As a result, pressing humanitarian needs in many other countries were left unaddressed. The experience of the 1990s suggests that global recession exacerbates donors' tendency to give according to domestic political interest, rather than according to humanitarian needs.

6

Resourcing humanitarian action in the twenty-first century

The growth in the number of those affected by disasters, explored in Chapter 2, will require an equivalent growth in humanitarian assistance. Indeed equivalent growth would be a bare minimum, simply maintaining the current (often inadequate) standards of response. To improve the *quality* of response for all affected people will cost considerably more, though not large amounts compared with other areas of government spending. And to fund longer-term solutions to humanitarian problems will cost still more, although in the long term it will save money that would otherwise be required for humanitarian response.

Fortunately, the proliferation of both institutions and donors from outside the Western humanitarian sphere provides real hope that some additional resources – and the additional capacity – can be found to help fund an adequate response to growing humanitarian need. If these non-OECD donors increased their contribution to a fair share of the humanitarian funding that is really needed, *and* if the OECD states that have been the main donors of most humanitarian aid did so too, *and* if they all gave their funds predictably, impartially, and accountably, then every person in need of humanitarian aid might reasonably expect to receive it. Those are quite a few 'ifs'. This chapter will look at what is needed to make them a reality.

What is required of humanitarian funding?

Adequate funding

The world spends very little of its wealth on humanitarian aid. International humanitarian aid was estimated to be $14.2bn in 2006.[165] That is less than the world spent on video games in the same year.[166] This figure includes contributions from donor governments, international organisations, members of the general public, and private companies (but

Who gives most generously in humanitarian crises?
Per capita spend on humanitarian aid by OECD countries in 2006

Per capita spend (US$)

Luxembourg	~93
Norway	~80
Sweden	~51
Denmark	~43
Netherlands	~32
Republic of Ireland	~25
Switzerland	~20
Finland	~17
UK	~11
Belgium	~8
US	~7
Australia	~6
Canada	~6
Germany	~5
Spain	~4
New Zealand	~4
Austria	~3
France	~3
Italy	~2
Greece	~1
Portugal	~1
Japan	~0.5

Source: OECD

does not include unrecorded aid or remittances from family members and diaspora communities). By contrast, military expenditure in 2006 was roughly 85 times that figure at around $1,300bn.[167]

Nevertheless, humanitarian aid grew significantly in the first few years of this century. Since the second half of the 1990s, humanitarian funding from the 23 donors who are members of the OECD's Development Assistance Committee (DAC) has doubled, to a total of just over $9bn in 2006.[168] The USA is the largest OECD donor: in 2006 it accounted for 35 per cent (just over $3bn) of the DAC humanitarian total, ahead of the UK, Germany, the Netherlands, and Sweden. Others outside the DAC, such as the Gulf states, are becoming increasingly important donors too.

While the amount of humanitarian aid has increased, however, much more money is required. According to new research for this report, by 2015 the numbers of people affected by climate-related disasters in an average year could increase by more than 50 per cent compared with the decade 1998–2007, bringing the annual average to more than 375 million people. This is not a precise prediction. It does however present a stark warning of the scale of humanitarian need that the world could face. Based on that projection, the world will have to spend around $25bn per year on humanitarian assistance in 2015, *just to maintain current levels of humanitarian response* – the equivalent of around $50 per affected person. If, as this report has argued, the quality of humanitarian response must be improved, and greater efforts made to address long-term vulnerability to disasters, $50 per affected person will be woefully inadequate. A reasonable response requires far higher per-capita spending.

In Bangladesh, where Cyclone Sidr destroyed or damaged 1.5 million homes in November 2007, affected families still lived underneath flimsy plastic sheeting and bits of cloth months later, because a government housing grant of $70 per family was not enough to enable them to rebuild their homes.[169]

Certainly the DAC donors could do much more than they do now. In 2006, if all DAC members had given as generously – in terms of spending per capita of their own populations – as the ten most generous DAC governments,[170] total DAC humanitarian assistance would have topped $36bn. And global humanitarian assistance would have exceeded $42bn, three times the actual figure. That total would have been enough to provide $154 for every person affected by emergencies.

China's ambassador to India, Zhang Yan (left) shakes hands with an Indian army officer as relief aid is loaded on board an Indian Air Force aircraft. The aid goods, donated by the Indian government, were destined for victims of the Sichuan earthquake, which killed an estimated 70,000 people in May 2008.

Manpreet Romana / AFP / Getty Images

All OECD DAC countries have committed to give 0.7 per cent of their gross national income (GNI) in official development assistance (ODA) by 2015. Humanitarian aid, meanwhile, accounts for around 9 per cent of overseas development aid.[171] If all DAC member states meet their 0.7 per cent development aid target, and maintain the current proportion of spending on emergencies, they would be giving 0.08 per cent of their GNI in humanitarian aid. The Netherlands, Denmark, Norway, Sweden, and Luxembourg already donate this amount or more.[172] If these five countries can demonstrate this level of concern for those affected by emergencies, it is surely within the means of all rich nations to do so.

There have been worrying indications that global ODA levels may actually be starting to fall.[173] In the light of the global economic crisis that began in 2008, and if aid levels follow the trend of the 1990s recession, this downward trend may be both sustained and significant (see figure p90). So, beyond the OECD DAC donors, what other sources of additional humanitarian funding exist in the world today?

The growth in non-OECD humanitarian donorship

Up to 12 per cent of money for the relief of disasters comes from states other than those in the OECD.[174] Aid from non-OECD donors is not new: Kuwait, Saudi Arabia, and many other Gulf states have provided aid in the form of soft loans and development assistance for over 40 years.[175] But countries such as China, Saudi Arabia, the United Arab Emirates, Turkey, and South Korea[176] are now contributing hundreds of millions of dollars to emergency relief. Turkey alone provided $150m in assistance to Pakistan following the earthquake in October 2005. In 2007, Saudi Arabia provided $100m in response to Cyclone Sidr in Bangladesh, representing some 53 per cent of the total humanitarian funding for the crisis, and pledged $500m in May 2008 to plug the World Food Program's funding gap.[177] The Indian Ocean tsunami in 2004 prompted donations from 77 non-DAC countries including Liberia, one of the world's least-developed countries.[178]

However, as can also be the case with aid from Western donors, non-DAC donors tend to contribute on the basis of strategic interest or public reaction, or they focus on emergencies that are perceived to be close, either geographically (South Africa gave over 80 per cent of its humanitarian aid to states in sub-Saharan Africa in 2007),[179] or in terms of culture or religion.

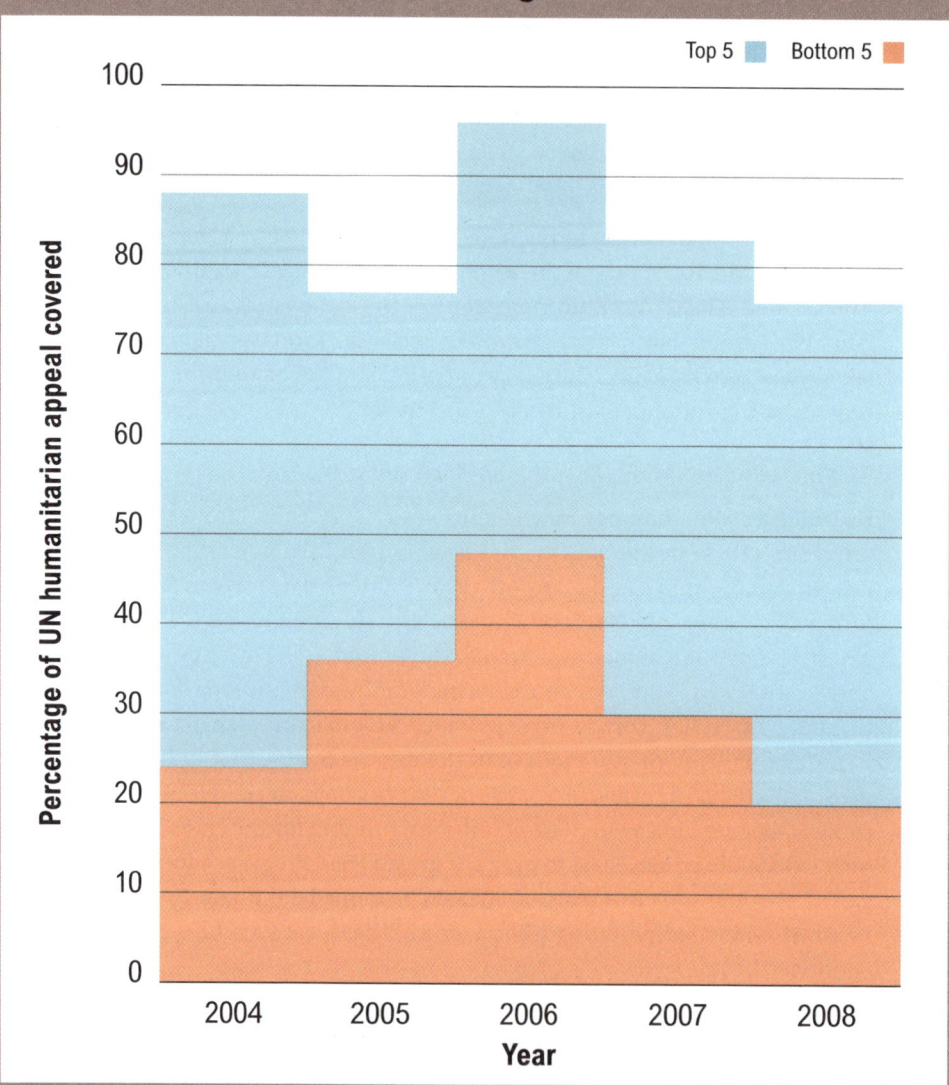

The shortfall in humanitarian appeals
The difference between the best and worst funded emergencies

Top 5 ■ Bottom 5 ■

Percentage of UN humanitarian appeal covered

Year

Source: OCHA FTS (Financial Tracking Service)

The initial targets for UN humanitarian appeals are very rarely met. The top 5 shown in this figure are the appeals in each year which received nearest to 100% of the funds sought for the emergencies represented; the bottom 5 are appeals which received nearest to 0%.

These non-DAC donors also tend to channel their aid outside international donor co-ordination mechanisms. In Bangladesh, following Cyclone Sidr in 2007, government officials and donors admitted to Oxfam that they had little information about the timeframe for spending Saudi Arabia's substantial bilateral contribution, or what activities they were funding.[180] This lack of clarity can lead to duplicate funding, or else leave substantial gaps in provision. Aid from non-traditional donor countries provides a significant opportunity to increase the funding for humanitarian aid in the twenty-first century, but – like aid from DAC countries – it will need to be better co-ordinated and distributed more impartially if it is to meet its full potential.

Impartial funding

How humanitarian aid is spent is as important as how much of it there is. To be effective, funds must be timely, adequate, and distributed impartially. Too often, it is none of these.

We are confronted daily with news of civilians fleeing sudden and catastrophic disasters or conflicts. However, many tens of millions of people are affected by slower, quieter, more insidious emergencies. Such forgotten emergencies are often those with the highest numbers of people affected. Yet the difference between the world's response to high-profile disasters and to chronic emergencies could not be starker; comparing the global response to the Indian Ocean tsunami in 2004 with the response to the conflict in Chad in the same year, the 500,000 people who received aid after the tsunami received an average of $1,241 each in official assistance, while the 700,000 recipients of aid in Chad received just $23 each.[181]

Of course, the cost of an adequate humanitarian response varies according to local conditions, accessibility, and market prices. But the vast disparities in the allocation of aid per recipient in response to different emergencies cannot simply be explained by variations in the cost of delivering assistance. There is much greater correlation between the public profile and political priority afforded to emergencies in donor states, and the amount of money allocated.

Recent years have seen the creation of pooled funds under UN stewardship, which aim to even out these disparities. By soliciting contributions to centralised humanitarian funds, the logic goes, allocations can be made by the UN on the basis of humanitarian need.

Funding for adaptation

Climate change is already endangering the lives and livelihoods of poor people in developing countries. Urgent assistance is therefore needed in order to help them to adapt to unavoidable climate change. This can involve, for example, the development of drought- or flood-tolerant crops, or training and equipment for rainwater harvesting to cope with altered rainfall patterns. It may include investments to build or improve infrastructure, like higher roads and bridges in flood-prone areas or modified buildings in areas increasingly struck by hurricanes. Community-based disaster risk reduction plans, insurance mechanisms, and social safety nets can help vulnerable people cope with increasing risks.

Oxfam estimates that poor countries need at least $50 billion a year of additional funding to meet the costs of adapting to unavoidable climate change. More will be needed unless global emissions are cut rapidly. This money must be distinct from Overseas Development Assistance, and not counted towards meeting the UN-agreed target of 0.7 per cent of Gross National Product for aid. On the 'polluter pays' principle, this money is owed as compensatory finance by rich, high-emitting countries to those most vulnerable to climate change. Rich countries' contributions should therefore be in the form of grants, not loans, and in line with their responsibility for causing climate change and their capability to assist. Adaptation finance must also be predictable, stable, and easily accessible.

Governments must agree on a global framework for adaptation that meets these criteria when they meet in Copenhagen at the end of 2009 to agree a new global deal on climate change. Oxfam has shown that sufficient, predictable, and stable revenues can be raised by auctioning a small proportion of the emissions allowances under a post-Kyoto international emissions trading scheme, and by the full auctioning of developed-country allowances under new emissions trading schemes for the aviation and shipping sectors.*

---

*Oxfam International (2008), 'Turning Carbon into Gold: How the international community can finance climate change adaptation without breaking the bank', Oxford: Oxfam International.

Currently, such pooled funding mechanisms include the Central Emergency Relief Fund (CERF), which is administered from UN OCHA, and the Common Humanitarian Funds (CHFs), which are allocated to each country, ready in case of emergency, and managed under UN leadership.

In the DRC, pooled funding has, on the face of it, increased the funding available to a historically chronically underfunded crisis. In 2006, the UN consolidated appeal for the DRC was so heavily underfunded that an allocation of $38m from the CERF was made in order to redress the shortfall.[182] In the same year, the new DRC CHF received some $90m in contributions – more than four times what was expected. Many donors, including the UK and Dutch governments, substantially increased their contributions to the pooled funds while also maintaining existing bilateral funding to NGOs and others.[183]

All this extra money should have resulted in much better quality and coverage of assistance for the citizens of the DRC. In late 2006, Oxfam asked more than 60 staff from humanitarian agencies, local NGOs, UN agencies, and other organisations to give their opinion on whether they thought the pooled funds had made a genuine difference.[184] The majority felt that there had been no significant increases in their annual budgets or programmes. They struggled to identify any concrete improvements for emergency-affected people.[185]

Innovations such as pooled funds must be judged on whether they bring about demonstrable improvements in the lives of those affected by disasters. Systems for monitoring and evaluating pooled funds must be far more transparent and robust – from the allocation of funding from bilateral donors, via the UN umbrella agencies, through to the implementation of aid projects on the ground.[186] UN agencies, in particular, have only very general reporting requirements. No common targets or indicators for success have been agreed, and there are no mandatory and comprehensive project impact assessments or evaluations. Despite attempts by UN OCHA to carry out more rigorous needs assessments in order to allocate funding accordingly, there is little baseline data to help gauge the impact of any improvements resulting from pooled funds or other aspects of UN system reform.

The logos of Oxfam and the European Commission Humanitarian Aid Office (ECHO) adorn a community washstand, constructed from recycled barrels, Camp Aero, Bunia, DRC. (2004)

Jane Beesley / Oxfam

Timely funding

As well as adequacy and impartiality, timeliness of funding is critical. In the gap between a catastrophe occurring and the launch of an effective humanitarian response, much preventable loss of life and livelihood occurs. Many donors have recognised this and have introduced fast-track mechanisms for the disbursal of humanitarian aid to agencies on the ground.

The European Commission Humanitarian Office's 'primary emergency' facility enables it to assess a crisis, allocate money, and disburse funds to implementing agencies within a matter of days, without multiple layers of decision-making. In the DRC, the UN's innovative Rapid Response Mechanism (RRM), administered by UNICEF and UN OCHA, pre-positions both funding and aid stocks with implementing agencies. When a crisis occurs, the RRM allows these agencies to respond in a matter of hours.

Too many mechanisms, presented as funding for first-phase emergency response, in reality, prove too slow and too bureaucratic to allow life-saving aid to be delivered within the timeframes required. In 2008, the CERF was not a practicable source of funding for the very first phase of humanitarian response.[187] This funding is channelled from UN OCHA to UN agencies (such as UNHCR, UNICEF, and the World Food Program), and then to non-UN implementing organisations. Once allocated to UN agencies, there is no shared timescale or method for funding to be disbursed to implementing agencies. In the DRC, agencies which received CERF money in 2006 confirmed that there was a delay of three to six months between the initial identification of need and the actual disbursement of funds.[188]

Some bilateral aid donors, such as the European Commission and the US government, have chosen to remain outside the CERF. Meanwhile, some participating bilateral humanitarian donors seem to believe that allocating funding to the CERF is a substitute for their own rapid-response capability, prompting them to reduce staff capacity accordingly.

Good Humanitarian Donorship

Donor governments are unlikely to improve funding practices if they do not become more accountable: to each other, to aid recipients, and to their publics.[189] Some 35 donor states (plus the European Commission) have signed up to the Good Humanitarian Donorship initiative (GHD),

Promises, promises ... What humanitarian donors have committed to do in funding emergency response

Many of the leading humanitarian donor governments have signed up to the 'principles and good practice of humanitarian donorship' (GHD). Through signing up to GHD, each donor government has promised (among other things) to:

- Be guided by the humanitarian principles of humanity, impartiality, neutrality, and independence;

- Support a range of humanitarian needs, including the protection of civilians and the provision of food, water and sanitation, shelter and health services;

- Respect and promote the implementation of international humanitarian law, refugee law, and human rights;

- Strive to ensure flexible and timely funding;

- Allocate humanitarian funding on the basis of identified need;

- Strengthen the capacity of affected countries and communities to prevent, prepare for, mitigate, and respond to humanitarian crises;

- Provide assistance in ways that are supportive of recovery and long-term development;

- Support and promote the central and unique role of the United Nations in providing leadership and co-ordination;

- Affirm the primary position of civilian organisations in implementing humanitarian action.

Source: www.goodhumanitariandonorship.org

which commits them to 23 principles. These include: funding according to need rather than political interest; working to improve assessment and the quality of humanitarian programmes; and respecting *and promoting* the implementation of international humanitarian law, refugee law, and human rights.[190]

GHD is a unique opportunity to improve funding practices and humanitarian aid quality. But it could have much broader and more fundamental implications for emergency-affected people; for instance, GHD principles could be read as a commitment to joint action between member donor states to challenge other governments that block access to civilian populations.[191]

GHD has so far failed to live up it its promise. For all its 23 principles, GHD donors have only agreed 17 performance indicators and no tangible targets or commitments to concrete institutional change. All but one of those indicators focus on how aid flows – through which funding mechanisms and to which agencies and countries – rather than on the actual impact of donors' policies and aid on the lives of affected people. There have been several excellent attempts to suggest improved GHD indicators, as well as an independent initiative – the 'Humanitarian Response Index' – set up to monitor donor performance against GHD principles.[192] The GHD itself, however, needs a much more comprehensive and tangible range of targets if it is to reach its potential.[193]

International humanitarian agencies have for the most part failed to recognise the potential of GHD and to hold donor governments to account for the commitments they have made.

GHD remains a club of Western donors. The GHD needs to widen its membership and engage non-OECD humanitarian donors on key issues such as impartiality, needs-based allocations, and predictability and flexibility of financing. More generally, too few non-traditional donors have taken part in international fora on humanitarian funding (such as the UN OCHA Donor Support Group). This is due to lack of effort on both sides. The huge 'unofficial' contribution to the relief of emergencies from non-DAC donors is therefore largely unrecognised by the UN, humanitarian agencies, or Western donors.

Volunteers from the Taiwan
Buddhist Tzu Chi Foundation
distributing food supplies door-to-
door to victims of the Cyclone
Nargis disaster in Burma/
Myanmar (2008).

Taiwan Buddhist Tzu Chi Foundation Malaysia

Increasing humanitarian capacity

The trend towards more localised disasters demands a greater number of local-level humanitarian actors. Fortunately, recent years have indeed seen a proliferation of non-state actors involved in the delivery of relief aid at both local and international levels, such as private companies and individuals, political parties, civil society, and religious groups.

The Malaysian Medical Relief Society (MERCY), for example, is just one of these new actors. Founded in 1999 as a direct response to the Kosovo crisis, it has quickly grown and is now present in emergencies across Asia and Africa. MERCY is a signatory to the Code of Conduct for the Red Cross and Red Crescent Movement and NGOs in Disaster Relief and the Sphere Standards in Humanitarian Aid, as well as being a member of the Humanitarian Accountability Partnership.[194]

While MERCY Malaysia may look and sound like many of its Western counterparts, others are carving their own distinctive and independent niche. Across the South China Sea in Taiwan is the headquarters of the Buddhist charitable organisation the Tzu Chi Foundation, with revenue of around $300m and 10 million supporters worldwide. The Foundation has responded to numerous emergencies across the region. While many Western NGOs were caught up in negotiations to work in Burma/Myanmar following Cyclone Nargis, the Tzu Chi Foundation was one of the first organisations providing assistance on the ground.

Many local agencies are non-partisan. Zakat committees,[195] for example, provide food aid, medical aid, and emergency cash for many living in the occupied Palestinian Territories of the West Bank and Gaza. During the second intifada, UN OCHA reported that the four largest Zakat committees alone provided food assistance to 145,450 households, making them the largest food donor in the occupied Palestinian Territories after UNRWA. Zakat committees do not discriminate on the basis of religion or political persuasion. Although they have effectively been criminalised by Israel on the basis of their close affiliation with Hamas, the Palestinian public do not see Zakat committees – many of which pre-date modern nationalist movements – as associated with any one political party.[196]

Many other non-state actors, however, do provide aid to a particular group defined by religion, ethnicity, or politics. This may simply reflect the homogeneous make-up of the community in which an organisation

Activists from an Islamic political party distribute food, medicine, and shelter in earthquake-hit southwest Pakistan (2008).

Banaras Khan / AFP / Getty Images

operates, but in some cases non-state groups are deliberately partisan in the delivery of relief assistance.

The solution however is not as simple as lecturing non-Western agencies about the need for impartiality. International humanitarian agencies will not be able to cope with the growth in humanitarian need without embracing the diverse group of agencies that already provides substantial amounts of relief. And given that the international humanitarian sector has been dominated by Western organisations, there is a danger that promoting 'universal' humanitarian principles like impartiality alongside quality standards may be seen as an imposition of Western principles and standards on non-Western actors. What is needed is for Western and non-Western agencies working together to create a more genuinely universal humanitarian purpose, pursuing traditional principles of impartiality and humanity in a way that speaks to every cultural and religious tradition.

For example, in recognition of the specific challenges facing Muslim NGOs and NGOs working in Muslim countries, three British NGOs (Islamic Relief, British Red Cross, and Oxfam) jointly set up the Humanitarian Forum.[197] This organisation is designed to foster co-operation among humanitarian and charitable organisations from Muslim countries or denominations on the one hand, and humanitarian and charitable organisations from the West and the multilateral system on the other. It provides training services for organisations in both the global North and South, facilitates partnerships, and promotes a well-regulated legal environment for both faith-based and non-faith-based NGOs in Muslim countries.

The private sector

Humanitarian action has always been dependent on the private sector to a certain extent – both for equipment and funds. Indeed, so varied are the types of relationships that may arise between humanitarian agencies and the private sector that it is difficult to make general statements. Individual shop owners and business-people in Burma/Myanmar spontaneously reacting in the aftermath of Cyclone Nargis can hardly be seen as analogous to multi-year, multi-million-dollar logistics partnerships between the World Food Program (WFP) and the global logistics giant TNT.

The clearest distinction is perhaps not one of scale, however, but between philanthropic and commercial activities. In philanthropic terms, there

TNT / WFP

Since 2002, TNT has been an active partner of the United Nations World Food Programme. To date, TNT has invested €38 million in the partnership in hands-on support in emergencies and training support to WFP.

was a significant increase in private-sector contributions to humanitarian appeals during the decade 1995–2005. In 2000, private companies together made up some 13.3 per cent of total humanitarian funding; by 2005, this share had risen to 24.4 per cent, although the majority of the increase can be attributed to the Indian Ocean tsunami.[198]

In addition to directly funding humanitarian appeals, many businesses want to engage their expertise more directly through longer-term partnerships with humanitarian agencies, donating goods and services in-kind. For business, partnership benefits may include enhanced goodwill, increased employee morale, and information sharing.[199] Perhaps the biggest benefit is positive publicity. In fact, engaging in corporate social responsibility initiatives involving humanitarian relief may simply be a way to enter new markets or to get access to new clients.[200] The fear of private companies profiting from supposedly humanitarian activities has been an emotive issue, and both sceptics and supporters of for-profits have been vocal in the debate. Nevertheless, the benefits of long-term partnerships with the private sector can be considerable for humanitarian agencies, bringing extra resources and skills as well as new practices and perspectives. Some private-sector actors are showing an increasing desire to go beyond even these roles in emergencies, and become humanitarian actors themselves.[201] Direct engagement by the private sector may remove the safeguards that apply when they are indirectly supporting humanitarian agencies or working in partnership with them. Private-sector actors bid to provide assistance mostly in accessible or marketable areas and for a profit or public-profile motive, not on the basis of need. Examples of local, national, and international private-sector humanitarian action have often been shown to lack understanding of or concern for humanitarian principles or standards.[202]

In reality this direct engagement in humanitarian activities remains extremely limited and is generally focused on large-scale reconstruction and development projects. But where private-sector actors do attempt to engage in disasters, it is imperative that those who engage their services require them to keep to commonly accepted humanitarian principles and standards – in particular that of impartiality. Whether those principles can ever be truly consistent with a profit-driven motive remains to be seen.

Members of the UN Security
Council cast their votes after the
review of the situation in Burma/
Myanmar, United Nations
Headquarters in New York (2007).

Eskinder Debebe / UN

A new humanitarian framework

If vulnerable people are to be adequately protected in an uncertain future, humanitarian assistance needs both the additional resources and the diverse additional capacity outlined above.

Every effort should be made to facilitate and encourage humanitarian aid flows from non-OECD donor states. All actors should recognise the important role of organisations from the global South in the provision of relief aid. At the same time, the principle of impartiality in humanitarianism must remain at the heart of all that humanitarian actors stand for. Established humanitarian actors – Western and non-Western – must work with new providers of relief in order to build adherence to universal humanitarian principles and standards.

Humanitarian agencies may find themselves making pragmatic choices to work alongside organisations that provide aid partially to particular groups, whether defined by religion, political affiliation, or ethnicity. Agencies should nevertheless be prepared to criticise such organisations where such practices undermine the rights to life and security of those who do not benefit.

So, we have seen that the world possesses the skills, knowledge, and experience required to safeguard lives in crisis. We also have sufficient financial and organisational resources to meet the challenge of humanitarian need in the twenty-first century. In the next chapter we bring all this together and look at what concrete action needs to be taken.

7

Building a safer future

The world must act now to reduce the numbers of people who will die or be made destitute by emergencies in the coming decades. Whether the world chooses to do so depends on the political will of states. And that depends on affected citizens demanding that their right to a secure life take precedence over all other concerns; and on people in rich countries pressing their governments to first, become more effective and more generous donors and second, to finance adaptation based on their historic responsibility for greenhouse gas emissions and their capability to pay.

Fundamental reforms are needed in these three key areas:

1 Building state responsibility for – and empowering vulnerable people to claim – the right to life;
2 Reducing vulnerability and mitigating threats over the long term;
3 Funding and improving international assistance by increasingly diverse humanitarian donors and agencies.

We will look at each of those priorities in turn.

Building state responsibility – and empowering vulnerable people

The primary focus of global humanitarian efforts must be to support states to safeguard the right to life of their own citizens. The increasing threat of localised emergencies demands a far greater focus on local accountability and response too. Much greater attention must be given by all parties to reinforcing *both* states' responsibilities to reduce long-term vulnerability by building human security, and to provide immediate assistance, *and* citizens' capacity to make forceful and effective claims on their governments to do so. In many cases, this will require a shift away from the historical focus on the duty and right of third parties – such as NGOs and the UN – to provide assistance.

Priorities for local civil-society organisations

In August 2008, up to 130,000 people were displaced in Georgia, in and around the disputed regions of South Ossetia and Abkhazia. For many affected civilians, it was not immediately clear what assistance they were entitled to or from whom. The Georgian Young Lawyers Association (GYLA) was one of only a handful of local civil-society organisations participating in the UN cluster meetings on civilian protection:

> Many displaced people do not know how to register, nor do they know of their rights. We are working with the national authorities in the registration of all internally displaced people...We are giving legal aid and providing legal representation to people affected.

Besarion Boxasvili (GYLA)[203]

Around the world, local civil-society organisations like GYLA, faith groups, and others can all play a vital mediating role between affected people and their governments. And local and international media can both inform and mobilise those affected by emergencies and monitor the government's response. But empowering citizens to claim life-saving humanitarian assistance depends on civil-society organisations' capacity to do so. Within the constraints that may exist in authoritarian or war-torn countries, local civil-society organisations should:

- Ensure that both they and those they represent are as informed as they can be about – and confident to advocate with state and local government for – affected people's rights in emergencies;
- Familiarise themselves with key instruments of international[204] and national law relating to the right to life;
- Strengthen their capacity to respond in emergencies.

Priorities for national governments

The majority of states lie on the spectrum between the two extremes of responding effectively and acting malignly towards citizens in emergencies. Governments must treat citizens not as passive recipients of welfare, but as active protagonists in the provision of emergency assistance and in efforts to reduce their own vulnerability to future disasters.

National governments must:

- Take practical measures to build up effective emergency preparedness and response capacity, including:
  - Strengthening local and national civil defence capacity to respond to disasters, working with local agencies such as national Red Cross/Crescent societies;
  - Create functional and well-resourced national disaster-management units. These should ensure that contingency plans, as well as early warning, effective communication, and community mobilisation mechanisms are in place at national, regional, and local levels;
  - Ensure that clear lines of responsibility are established for emergencies and that, *inter alia*, relevant government ministries and military agencies co-ordinate their activities effectively; and
  - Enact effective, accountable, rights-based legislation to safeguard the right to life in times of national emergency – making reference to key instruments in international law and custom concerning humanitarian assistance.
- Take proactive steps to reduce long-term vulnerability, including tackling the risks from environmental hazards, and investing in sustainable livelihoods (see below);
- Allow space for, and be responsive to, requests and complaints relating to assistance from emergency-affected people and the civil-society organisations that represent or work with them; and
- Give the protection of civilians – like the provision of humanitarian assistance – the highest possible priority in every war or counter-insurgency strategy. For more detail on precise recommendations to protect civilians, see Oxfam's companion report 'For a Safer Tomorrow'.[205]

Priorities for multilateral action

Governments, acting both bilaterally and through multilateral organisations, also have a clear duty to support other states to realise the right to life and security – through exerting diplomatic pressure, as well as by offering financial aid and technical assistance.

Bilateral relationships – such as those between donor and recipient governments – and working through the UN are vital in this respect. However, regional bodies, such as the African Union, the Association of South East Asian Nations (ASEAN), and the Southern African Development

Community, will be playing an increasingly important role. These organisations may in many cases be better placed than donor governments or the UN, both to understand and respond to regional challenges and to support the rights of the citizens of their member states. Yet, currently, many regional organisations have no credible policy or operational capacity to support the humanitarian response or risk-reduction measures of their member states. They must, where necessary, strengthen regional agreements and capacity to do so.

The United Nations itself has a long way to go – to improve both the performance of its humanitarian co-ordination in most crises, and the forcefulness of its mediation and diplomacy to encourage governments to respect their citizens' rights.

The UN Security Council must be prepared to demand the right of unfettered and unmolested humanitarian access by impartial humanitarian organisations, where states are unable or unwilling to sufficiently assist and protect their citizens. The Security Council must be fully prepared to act in a timely and effective manner to exert diplomatic pressure on states (and non-state actors) that fail to safeguard life. It must be willing, as a last resort, to impose targeted sanctions on states that fail to exercise responsible sovereignty by wilfully causing the deaths of civilians, either by negligent or deliberate acts.

In doing so, they must of course find the most pragmatic solutions that best safeguard the right to life of affected populations – and not engage in fruitless condemnation of a national government's failures. They must recognise that the threat of sanction – and in particular, use of military force – may not be the best way forward. Indeed, the use of foreign military forces to provide aid in these circumstances will very rarely be useful. In May 2008, invoking the 'Responsibility to Protect' proved an unhelpful gambit following Cyclone Nargis, which devastated part of Burma/Myanmar. The quietly pragmatic approach of ASEAN, with other international diplomacy, ultimately elicited a more positive, if far from ideal, outcome for affected populations in the Irrawaddy Delta.

The UN should:

- Advocate much more strongly in-country for national governments to safeguard the rights to life and security of their citizens in situations of emergency;
- Support the claims of affected people to assistance from their government, opening up co-ordination mechanisms to them and building effective mechanisms to report failures and abuse by all humanitarian actors and to obtain redress;
- Encourage national governments to take a greater role in humanitarian co-ordination mechanisms;
- Ensure the demonstrable impartiality of humanitarian aid by maintaining clear separation between humanitarian aid and political/military objectives, including in the UN's integrated missions.

Priorities for international humanitarian agencies

International humanitarian agencies must work much more consistently to build states' capacity to discharge their responsibilities towards their citizens – as well as citizens' capacity to demand that their rights are respected. International humanitarian agencies must:

- Work with and through government agencies at local and national levels, wherever possible, to reinforce their capacity to respond in emergencies and reduce people's vulnerability;
- Empower emergency-affected communities to demand that governments, non-state actors, and others fulfil their obligations to save lives and build long-term human security. This includes building mechanisms by which emergency-affected people can effectively challenge failure – including failures by international NGOs themselves;
- Provide skills and tools for local civil-society organisations – including national non-government bodies like Red Cross and Red Crescent Societies – so that they can respond to and prepare for emergencies, as well as advocating with governments to do the same.

Reducing vulnerability and mitigating threats

While the threat from climate-related and other hazards will grow in the twenty-first century, it is the extent of people's vulnerability to those hazards that will determine how many lives will be lost. Far greater emphasis needs to be given to support states to take long-term action to reduce risks posed by factors such as long-term food insecurity, and environmental threats such as flooding, tropical storms, and earthquakes.

Governments, international humanitarian agencies, and local civil society must recognise the limitations of providing relief, and address the underlying causes of human vulnerability, whether they be environmental, technological, political, or economic.

Priorities for national action

Governments should:

- Invest in sustainable livelihoods so that people are more secure in terms of income and food. African governments should meet their NEPAD/CAADP[206] commitment to spend 10 per cent of national budgetary resources on developing the agricultural sector. They should invest in public services (in particular water supply, sanitation, and medical services) and infrastructure so that public-health risks are reduced;

- Make every effort to enact the commitments made under the Hyogo international strategy for disaster risk-reduction. In particular, they should adopt a disaster risk-reduction policy that allows communities to become more resilient to the threats they face, and they should invest in disaster preparedness, mitigation, and response;

- Improve urban planning and environmental policy and practice so that people living in slums are housed in more disaster-resistant dwellings and in areas that are less subject to environmental risk factors;

- Take urgent action to mitigate against climate change and finance adaptation where such action is too late. In accordance with their responsibilities and capabilities, rich countries must:

  - lead in cutting greenhouse-gas emissions so that global average temperature increases stay as far below 2°C as possible, and

– provide the finance needed for international adaptation to climate
change, channelling at least $50bn per year to poor countries. For
further details, see the Oxfam Briefing Paper, 'Climate Wrongs and
Human Rights'.[207]

Priorities for international action

• Donors and humanitarian agencies should strengthen the links between
relief and development, between emergency and reconstruction, and
between response and preparedness programming. Donors should
strengthen multi-annual funding streams to enhance predictability and
sustainability;

• Humanitarian agencies must work towards reducing vulnerability
where possible. Even if humanitarian organisations' mandate does not
extend beyond life-saving aid, they should still try to avoid using short-
term relief mechanisms – such as in-kind food aid – to respond to long-
term problems;

• International agencies should actively invest in disaster risk-reduction
capacity and programming, if their mandate includes recovery and
development. Disaster risk-reduction programmes should be integrated
with the work of Southern governments and donors in a way that helps
communities to propose their own solutions. International donors
must significantly increase funding of disaster preparedness,
mitigation, and response capacity without reducing other development
or humanitarian aid budgets.

• Funds for climate change adaptation should be delivered through a UN
adaptation finance mechanism responsible for oversight and delivery
and with a focus on the perspectives and needs of those communities
most vulnerable to climate change. The best way to achieve such a
mechanism under the governance of the parties to the UN Framework
Convention on Climate Change is to maintain and bolster the
Adaptation Fund.

Funding and improving international assistance

The overall amount of funding available for global efforts to save lives in emergencies as well as to reduce vulnerability must increase. Donors must provide humanitarian aid impartially, according to need – and be more willing to challenge the abuse of aid by others. They must also provide aid money in as timely, efficient, transparent, and accountable a way as possible.

Every effort must be made to facilitate and encourage humanitarian aid flows from non-traditional donor states. Humanitarian action must work on a more localised model in order to respond effectively in a changing world. This will demand a greater diversity of humanitarian actors, working at international, regional, and local levels.

The right to *good-quality* humanitarian assistance, which genuinely protects and preserves life, must be strengthened. Humanitarian projects must be better assessed and targeted and meet appropriate standards. They must be more sensitive to conflict and vulnerability and take better account of underlying threats. They must be more accountable to the people whose right to life they are supposed to protect, and must reinforce the accountability between citizens and states in emergencies.

Priorities for international action

Donor governments:

- Must increase the volume of humanitarian assistance, both to overcome the huge current shortfalls, and to prepare for the more than 375 million people who may be affected by climate-related disasters, and the tens of millions more by conflict, by 2015. That will require far more than the $25bn a year that would simply provide today's inadequate level of aid to those millions of people. Indeed, a commitment to spending $42bn a year – which would be perfectly possible if all OECD governments acted like their ten most generous members – would be a vital first step;
- Should work towards a target of giving 0.08 per cent of their GNI as humanitarian aid (as part of their commitment to providing 0.7 per cent in total ODA). Countries like Japan, France, Germany, and the USA in particular must give a higher percentage of their GNI than at present;

- Must ensure that money for humanitarian relief is allocated impartially across different crises, according to need rather than political, military, or domestic priorities;
- Should continue to support and invest in UN pooled funding mechanisms at current levels, but should be prepared to demand evidence of real, demonstrable impact on affected communities;
- Should ensure they retain and strengthen their bilateral fast-response funding mechanisms, upholding the diversity of funding mechanisms (rather than centralising all humanitarian funding through the UN); and
- Should sign up to and uphold the principles of the Good Humanitarian Donorship initiative. Donors who are part of the GHD should be prepared to hold each other to account, and also to establish independent accountability within the initiative. DAC and non-DAC donors should debate principles and standards together, as well as embracing good practice as it evolves, and enhancing transparency, effectiveness, accountability, and predictability.

International humanitarian organisations must:
- Reassert their core principles of impartiality and independence, by making sure that their own activities are rigorously impartial, and by vigorously advocating against the abuse of humanitarian aid;
- Ensure that assistance is given on the basis of solid and vulnerability-sensitive needs assessment, using appropriate standards such as the Sphere Minimum Standards, and holding other signatories to account;
- Ensure that women as well as men are actively involved in the design, targeting, and implementation of humanitarian activities;
- Increase their accountability and transparency to aid recipients and local stakeholders as well as to donors and each other; and
- Carry out a rigorous and context-specific analysis of the populations they set out to support and ensure that projects are sensitive to particular vulnerabilities, as well as to conflict.

The UN must:
- Prioritise leadership of country-level co-ordination, speeding up their efforts to improve Humanitarian Coordinator recruitment, training, and support;
- Stop the practice of combining the role of UN Humanitarian Coordinator with other key UN roles, such as the UN Resident Coordinator;

- Ensure UN cluster leads have adequate technical capacity and co-ordination skills. The UN Humanitarian Coordinator must hold UN cluster leads in-country to account for their performance;
- Ensure that a 'fire wall' is maintained between the management of political and military peacekeeping operations and the UN's humanitarian functions, even in integrated missions. In each country, OCHA should have a separate and independent presence from the UN political arm (the Department of Political Affairs) and peacekeeping mission (the Department of Peacekeeping Operations);
- Attract non-traditional humanitarian donors to be incorporated in international humanitarian donor co-ordination mechanisms, such as the OCHA donor support group; and
- Continue to develop and improve pooled funding mechanisms, such as the CERF. The evaluation of these mechanisms should focus on real, concrete impact on recipients. These should be administered consistently, as well as being transparent, accountable, and timely. They must support both initial assessment and first-phase response. The length of time taken for funds to be expedited from UN agencies to emergencies on the ground should be greatly reduced.

Evans Garcon uses a community water tap in Cap Haitian, Haiti. Oxfam has worked with local authorities to reduce the threat to lives posed by a combination of urban poverty and frequent floods. Part of Oxfam's approach has been to protect local water sources vulnerable to contamination due to flooding.

Abbie Trayler-Smith / Oxfam

Conclusion

Five years ago our lives were very difficult. Now things are better. Though there's been little rain, we have built embankments in our field. Our situation has improved. We are planting our land and, because of this, we have our dignity.

Shanti Devi, Bundelkhand, India, 2008[208]

There is nothing inevitable about a future in which greater numbers of people die and are made destitute by natural hazards and conflict. In a future of climate change, rising hazard and a proliferation of disasters, the world can still mitigate threats and reduce people's vulnerability to them. Many governments, humanitarian organisations, and communities are already doing this – but not nearly enough.

It all comes down to choice – primarily by national governments. The most critical factor in deciding whether or not governments choose to safeguard life and address vulnerability will be whether they see it as in their interest to do so. The moral case comes from every major world religion's prescription to look after fellow human beings in need. The legal case comes from international legal instruments. But whether governments choose to act in accordance with moral obligation and legal duty will depend on their calculation of their self-interest – and the pressure that is brought to bear on them.

Most critically, this pressure must come from empowered citizens demanding respect for their rights in crisis. It must also come from courageous and assertive local civil-society organisations acting as mediators between citizens and states – as indeed they do in many instances, from Indonesia to Malawi, and from India to Georgia. And it must come from people everywhere waking up to the dramatic increase in humanitarian needs, and deciding to do something about it. As soon as 2015, the growth of climate-driven emergencies will affect substantially more people. But because many of these new crises will not be dramatic enough to grab the attention of global media or even national authorities, there is a very real danger that the world will not even notice this rising tide of humanitarian need, and that millions of people will, unnecessarily, lose their lives or livelihoods.

Rabeya creates a mud bank in front of her house as a protection against flood water in Bogra, Bangladesh. Rabeya has experienced flooding many times, but says that the floods of 2007 were extreme.

Abir Abdullah / epa / Corbis

International humanitarian organisations have a vital role to play, both in supporting governments to fulfil their responsibilities and in supporting civil society to demand that they do so. International humanitarian organisations must provide impartial, accountable, and effective assistance in order to save lives. In terms of accountability and consistent performance, they too have a long way to go to meet the standard that people affected by emergencies have a right to expect. In today's world – and tomorrow's – this will require an international humanitarian sector that is determined to continue to improve and is united on universal principles of impartiality and humanity, while reflecting an increasing diversity of humanitarian agencies from many cultures and traditions.

Governments worldwide must support each other to safeguard lives through effective and impartial humanitarian aid and financing for adaptation, and hold each other to account when they fail, through multilateral organisations, both regional and global. Rich countries, including emerging donors far beyond the traditional OECD, must make a far bigger investment in humanitarian aid – far beyond the $25bn a year that would simply allow donors to stand still by 2015 in terms of the quality and contribution to each affected person. Far more than that will be needed to improve humanitarian aid as the need for it grows substantially. Indeed, far more will be needed than the $42bn that could be provided simply by all OECD governments behaving like their ten most generous members. Even in difficult economic times, the world can afford these figures and more, and must rise to that challenge to prevent a far greater loss of life in humanitarian emergencies in the future.

It is too late to prevent the twenty-first century from being one of immense humanitarian need (though the scale of that is in the hands of governments and others tackling climate change and other causes).

It is *not* too late to provide a decent humanitarian response and to reduce the risks of vulnerable people succumbing to the climate-related and other shocks that the coming years will bring.

Whether or not there is the will to do that will be one of the defining features of our century – and will determine whether millions of vulnerable people live or die. That is the humanitarian challenge of the twenty-first century.

Notes

1   The causes and impact of disasters are often anything but natural. Disasters are the interaction of environmental shocks (storms, floods, and droughts) with human vulnerability (who one is, where one lives, and how one makes a living) creating risk: the danger of losing life and livelihood. Other exacerbating factors include environmental mismanagement, such as the failure to maintain infrastructure such as dams and flood defences.

2   For details of this projection please see 'Forecasting the numbers of people affected annually by natural disasters up to 2015', internal Oxfam study, April 2009 www.oxfam.org

3   United Nations (2007) *Disaster Risk Reduction: Global Review 2007*, p. 25.

4   D. Smith and J. Vivekananda (2007) 'A Climate of Conflict: the Links between Climate Change, Peace and War', London: International Alert, www.international-alert.org/climate_change.php.

5   See the University of Uppsala Conflict Data Programme, www.pcr.uu.se/research/UCDP/index.htm (last accessed November 2008).

6   Last available figures. Throughout this report, figures are in US dollars unless otherwise stated.

7   For Europe-wide bail-out, see 'EU leaders endorse continent-wide bailout', CBS News, 15 October 2008, www.cbsnews.com/stories/2008/10/15/world/main4524028.shtml?source=RSSattr=Business_4524028 (last accessed November 2008). For Hypo Real Estate example, see 'Germany clinches bank rescue deal', BBC News, 6 October 2008, http://news.bbc.co.uk/1/hi/business/7653868.stm (last accessed November 2008). For the Royal Bank of Scotland example, see 'UK banks receive £37bn bail-out', BBC News, 13 October 2008, http://news.bbc.co.uk/1/hi/business/7666570.stm (last accessed November 2008).

8   Oxfam International (2008) 'Haiti situation "at breaking point"', press release, 8 September 2008, www.oxfamamerica.org/whatwedo/where_we_work/camexca/news_publications/the-water-started-to-rise-and-it-did-not-stop (last accessed November 2008).

9   UN Stabalisation Mission in Haiti (2008) 'Gonaïves, deux semaines après le déluge!', www.reliefweb.int/rw/rwb.nsf/db900sid/RMOI-7JNJMU?OpenDocument&rc=2&cc=hti (last accessed November 2008).

10   IFRC (2007) 'Climate Change and the International Federation', background note distributed to IFRC national societies.

11   S. Dercon (2004) 'Growth and shocks', *Journal of Development Economics* 74(2): 309–29.

12   Christian Aid (2007) 'Human Tide: the Real Migration Crisis', London: Christian Aid, www.christianaid.org.uk/stoppoverty/climatechange/resources/human_tide.aspx (last accessed November 2008).

13   Asian Development Bank (2004) 'Fighting Poverty in Asia and the Pacific: The Poverty Reduction Strategy of the Asian Development Bank', www.adb.org/Documents/Policies/Poverty_Reduction/mission.asp?p=policies (accessed November 2008).

14   I. MacAuslan (2008) 'India's National Rural Empolyment Guarantee Act: a case study for how change happens', background paper for D. Green (2008) *From Poverty to Power*, Oxford: Oxfam International. See www.fp2p.org.

15   Reuters (2008) 'Vast Chile volcano ash cloud partially collapses', 13 May 2008, www.reliefweb.int/rw/rwb.nsf/db900sid/KHII-7EM89T?OpenDocument&rc=2&cc=chl (last accessed November 2008).

16   Interview with Jane Beesley, Oxfam GB, March 2008.

17   Interview with Marie Cacace, Oxfam GB, August 2008.

18   *Ibid.*

19   Ban Ki-moon (2007) 'Secretary-General's Report on the Protection of Civilians in Armed Conflict', *op.cit.*

20   Figures compiled from UN consolidated appeals data, see www.humanitarianappeal.net (last accessed November 2008).

21   Unpublished research carried out for Oxfam GB's Humanitarian Department.

22   For more information on this project, see www.oxfam.org.uk/oxfam_in_action/impact/success_stories/bolivia_farming.html (last accessed November 2008).

23   See PricewaterhouseCoopers (2007) 'Entertainment and Media Outlook 2007-11', http://www.pwc.co.uk/eng/publications/global_entertainment_and_media_outlook_2007_2011.html (last accessed November 2008).

24   Figures derived from UN OCHA's Financial Tracking Service (FTS), http://ocha.unog.ch/fts2/ (last accessed November 2008) and UN Consolidated Appeal documents, www.humanitarianappeal.net (last accessed November 2008).

25   Oxfam International (2008) 'For a Safer Tomorrow: Protecting Civilians in a Multipolar World', Oxford: Oxfam International.

26   Oxfam International (2008) 'Climate Wrongs and Human Rights: Putting People at the Heart of Climate Change Policy', Oxford: Oxfam International.

27   The number of people currently estimated to be affected by emergencies is 272 million, according to the Humanitarian Futures Programme (2008) *op.cit.*

28   See the University of Uppsala Conflict Data Programme, www.pcr.uu.se/research/UCDP/index.htm (last accessed November 2008).

29   International Rescue Committee (2008) 'Mortality in the Democratic Republic of Congo: An Ongoing Crisis', www.theirc.org/resources/2007/2006-7_congomortalitysurvey.pdf (last accessed November 2008). Figure calculated on the basis of 727,000 'excess deaths' between January 2006 and April 2007.

30   R. Mountain, UN Humanitarian Coordinator for the DRC, in the forward to OCHA (2006) 'Action Plan 2006 DRC', http://ochadms.unog.ch/quickplace/cap/main.nsf/h_Index/2006_DRC_ActionPlan/$FILE/2006_DRC_ActionPlan_SCREEN.PDF?OpenElement (last accessed November 2008).

31   International Rescue Committee (2008) *op.cit.*

32   UNDP (2008) *Human Development Report 2008,* New York: UNDP.

33   For details on the humanitarian consequences, see OCHA (2008) 'Revision of the Kenya Emergency Humanitarian Response Plan 2008', http://ochaonline.un.org/humanitarianappeal/webpage.asp?Page=1662 (last accessed November 2008). The figure for estimated deaths is from the BBC, http://news.bbc.co.uk/1/hi/in_depth/africa/2008/kenya/default.stm (last accessed November 2008).

34   Interview with Jane Beesley, Oxfam GB, April 2008.

35   Institute for Public Policy Research (2008) 'Shared Destinies: Security in a Globlaised World', the interim report of the IPPR Commission on National Security in the 21st Century, London: IPPR, p. 57.

36   OCHA (2007) 'Mexico: Tabasco Floods OCHA Situation Report No.1', 3 November, www.reliefweb.int/rw/RWB.NSF/db900SID/RMOI-78MMQ9?OpenDocument (last accessed November 2008).

37   Quoted in *The Guardian* (2005) 'Climate Change Disaster is Upon Us, Warns UN', 5 October 2007, www.guardian.co.uk/environment/2007/oct/05/climatechange (last accessed November 2008).

38   C. Padmanabhan (2008) 'Embankments – or should we say entombments', *The Hindu*, 18 September 2008, www.thehindu.com/2008/09/19/stories/2008091956231100.htm (last accessed November 2008).

39   J. Guyler Delva (2008) 'Aid groups struggle after deadly storms in Haiti', Reuters AlertNet, 8 September 2008, www.alertnet.org/thenews/newsdesk/N08483383.htm (last accessed November 2008).

40   Oxfam (2008) 'Oxfam warns millions more Ethiopians going hungry as aid effort stalls', press release, www.oxfam.org.uk/applications/blogs/pressoffice/?p=1834 (last accessed November 2008).

41   For further details please see 'Forecasting the numbers of people affected annually by natural disasters up to 2015', internal Oxfam study, April 2009, available at www.oxfam.org

42   D. Maxwell, P. Webb, J. Coates, and J. Wirth (2008) 'Rethinking Food Security in Humanitarian Response', paper presented to the Food Security Forum in Rome, 16–18 April 2008.

43   Interview with Nicki Bennett, Oxfam GB, January 2008.

44   Pew Centre on Global Climate Change (2008) 'Hurricanes and Global Warming FAQs', www.pewclimate.org/hurricanes.cfm#2008 (last accessed November 2008).

45   Inter-governmental Panel on Climate Change (2007) 'Fourth Assessment Report' (Synthesis Report), www.ipcc.ch/ipccreports/ar4-syr.htm (last accessed November 2008), p. 46.

46   P.M. Cox, R.A. Betts, C.D. Jones, S.A. Spall, and I.J. Totterdell (2000) 'Acceleration of global warming due to carbon-cycle feedbacks in a coupled climate model', *Nature* 408: 184–7.

47   United Nations (2007) 'Disaster Risk Reduction Global Review', p. 19 (using data from the Centre for Research on the Epidemiology of Disasters (CRED) EM-DAT database).

48   *Ibid.*, p. 25

49   *Ibid.*, pp. 18–28.

50   D. Smith and J. Vivekananda (2007) *op.cit.*

51   Ban Ki-moon (2007) 'A Climate Culprit in Darfur', the *Washington Post*, 16 June 2007, www.washingtonpost.com/wp-dyn/content/article/2007/06/15/AR2007061501857.html (accessed November 2008).

52   Interview with Jane Beesley, Oxfam GB, August 2007.

53   United Nations (2007) *op.cit.*, pp. 19, 21.

54   IFRC (2007) *op.cit.*

55   Oxfam International (2008) 'Rethinking Disasters', New Delhi: Oxfam International, www.oxfam.org.uk/resources/policy/conflict_disasters/oxfam_india_rethinking_disasters. html (last accessed November 2008), p. 3.

56   US Congressman Elijah Cummings quoted in BBC (2005) 'Hurricane prompts awkward questions', 4 September, http://news.bbc.co.uk/2/hi/americas/4210648.stm (last accessed November 2008).

57   Interview with Jane Beesley, Oxfam GB, June 2007.

58   IRIN (2007) 'Tomorrow's Crisis Today', IRIN in-depth report, www.irinnews.org/InDepthMain.aspx?InDepthId=63&ReportId=73996 (last accessed November 2008).

59   *Ibid.*

60   A. Giridharadas (2005) 'Flood toll near 900 in Indian Monsoon', *International Herald Tribune*, 30 July, www.iht.com/articles/2005/07/29/news/india.php (last accessed November 2008).

61   P. Kapadia (2005) 'Mumbai's looming ecological disaster', BBC News, 2 August, http://news.bbc.co.uk/1/hi/world/south_asia/4737153.stm (last accessed November 2008).

62   D. Satterthwaite, S. Huq, H. Reid, M. Pelling, and P. Romero Lankao (2007) 'Adapting to Climate Change in Urban Areas', London: IIED.

63   Small Arms Survey (2007) *Small Arms Survey 2007: Arms and the City*, Cambridge: Cambridge University Press, p. 161.

64   O. Ryan (2008) 'Food riots grip Haiti', *The Guardian*, 9 April, www.guardian.co.uk/world/2008/apr/09/11 (last accessed November 2008).

65   Oxfam (2004) 'Ethiopia Food Security Assessment', unpublished internal paper.

66   Interview with Jane Beesley, Oxfam GB, July 2003.

67   FAO (2008) 'Briefing Paper: Hunger on the Rise', 17 September, www.fao.org/newsroom/common/ecg/1000923/en/hungerfigs.pdf (last accessed November 2008).

68   'India Child Malnourishment Rates Worse than Africa', 21 February 2007, quoting Indian Ministry of Health 'National Family Health Survey', January 2007.

69   Oxfam International (2006) 'Causing Hunger: an Overview of the Food Crisis in Africa', Oxford: Oxfam International, www.oxfam.org.uk/resources/policy/conflict_disasters/ downloads/bp91_hunger.pdf (last accessed February 2008).

70   Interview with Jane Beesley, Oxfam GB, Janurary 2004.

71   UNHCR (2008) 'Global Trends: Refugees, Asylum-seekers, Returnees, Internally Displaced and Stateless Persons', www.unhcr.org/statistics/STATISTICS/4852366f2.pdf (last accessed November 2008).

72   N. Myers (2005) 'Environmental Refugees: an Emergent Security Issue', paper for the 13th Economic Forum, Organisation for Security and Cooperation in Europe, Prague, 23–27 May, www.osce.org/documents/eea/2005/05/14488_en.pdf (last accessed February 2008).

73   For a detailed breakdown of the types of population 'push' factors which contribute to the figure of 1 billion, see Chirstian Aid (2007) *op.cit.*

74   Interview with Jane Beesley, Oxfam GB, March 2008.

75   See also R.J. Hardcastle and A.T.L. Chua (1998) 'Humanitarian assistance: towards a right of access to victims of natural disasters', *International Review of the Red Cross* 325: 589–609, www.icrc.org/web/eng/siteeng0.nsf/html/57JPJD (last accessed November 2008). See particularly note 47.

76   Article 3: 'Everyone has the right to life, liberty and security of person.' See Universal Declaration of Human Rights, G.A. res. 217A (III), (1948).

77   Preamble to the Universal Declaration of Human Rights.

78   R. Stoffels (2004) 'Legal regulation of humanitarian assistance in armed conflict: achievements and gaps', *International Review of the Red Cross* 855: 517.

79   *Ibid.*

80   Protocol Additional to the Geneva Conventions of 12 August 1949, and relating to the Protection of Victims of International Armed Conflicts (Protocol 1), 8 June 1977 Article 70(1).

81   J.M. Henckaerts and L. Doswald-Beck (2005) *Customary International Humanitarian Law*, Cambridge: Cambridge University Press.

82   The International Criminal Court has found that the 'creation of a humanitarian crisis' linked to crimes of terror and forcible transfers, *in combination* count as crimes against humanity as 'inhumane acts and persecution' – Prosecutor v. Radislav Krstic (Trial Judgement) [2001] IT-98-33, para 615.

83   Interview with Jane Beesley, Oxfam GB, March 2008.

84   K. Haver (2008) 'Out of Site: Building Better Responses to Displacement in the Democratic Republic of Congo by Helping Host Families', Oxfam International Research Report, Oxford: Oxfam International.

85   K. Savage and P. Harvey (2007) 'Remittances During Crises: Implications for Humanitarian Response', Humanitarian Policy Group Briefing Paper No. 26, London: Overseas Development Institute.

86   IFRC (2008) 'Red Crescent Society of Kyrgyzstan first to respond to quake survivors', press release, 7 October, www.ifrc.org/docs/news/08/08100701/ (last accessed November 2008).

87   General Assembly Resolution 43/131 of 1989 affirms 'the primary responsibility of states to provide assistance to victims of natural disasters and other similar emergencies that occur within their territory'.

88   B. Kendall (2008) 'Can disasters shape history?', BBC News, 5 June, http://news.bbc.co.uk/1/hi/world/7436510.stm (last accessed November 2008).

89   *Ibid.*

90   CBS News (2005) 'Poll: Katrina response inadequate', www.cbsnews.com/stories/2005/09/08/opinion/polls/main824591.shtml (last accessed November 2008).

91   CBS News (2008) 'CBS Poll: Public Backs GOP's Gustav Change', www.cbsnews.com/stories/2008/09/02/opinion/polls/main4408967.shtml (last accessed November 2008).

92   D. Green (2008) *From Poverty to Power: How Active Citizens and Effective States Can Change the World*, Oxford: Oxfam International.

93   UNDRO (1992) *Directory of National Emergency Response Offices, Disaster Emergency Plans and Legislation, and Regional and Sub-Regional Agreements for Disaster Assistance*, New York: UNDRO. The directory lists the legislation of 64 countries.

94   Reuters (2008) 'Vast Chile volcano ash cloud partially collapses', Reuters, 13 May, www.reliefweb.int/rw/rwb.nsf/db900sid/KHII-7EM89T?OpenDocument&rc=2&cc=chl (last accessed November 2008).

95   Quoted in M. Thompson and I. Gaviria (2004) 'Cuba Weathering the Storm: Lessons in Risk Reduction from Cuba, an Oxfam America Report', Boston: Oxfam America.

96   J. Bevan (2002) 'National Hurricane Center Tropical Cyclone Report: Hurricane Michelle, 29 October–5 November 2001', www.nhc.noaa.gov/2001michelle.html (last accessed November 2008).

97   I. MacAuslan (2008) *op.cit.*

98   Oxfam International (2008) 'Climate Wrongs and Human Rights', *op.cit.*

99   Oxfam International (2007) 'Adapting to climate change: what's needed in poor countries, and who should pay', Oxford: Oxfam International.

100   J. Dreze and C. Oldiges (2007) 'Commendable Act', *Frontline* 24 (14).

101   'NREGA: Dismantling the contractor raj', *The Hindu,* 20 November 2007, www.hindu.com/2007/11/20/stories/2007112056181000.htm (last accessed November 2008).

102   'The real radicalism of NREGA', *The Hindu,* 22 May 2008, www.hindu.com/2008/05/22/stories/2008052253871000.htm (last accessed November 2008).

103   Interview with Jane Beesley, Oxfam GB, March 2008.

104   The Economist Intelligence Unit (2007) 'Dominican Republic Politics: Disaster Strikes', 6 November, www.viewswire.com/index.asp?layout=VWArticleVW3&article_id=162750801&region_id=&country_id=920000292&channel_id=210004021&category_id=500004050&refm=vwCat&page_title=Article&rf=0 (last accessed November 2008).

105   Ban Ki-moon (2007) 'Secretary-General's Report on the Protection of Civilians in Armed Conflict', *op.cit.*

106   OCHA (2008), 'Gaza Humanitarian Situation Report', 17 November 2008, http://www.ochaopt.org/documents/ocha_opt_gaza_situation_report_2008_11_17.pdf (last accessed December 2008)

      For cash for work, see Financial Times (2008), 'Banks in Gaza shut as Israel chokes cash flow', Financial Times, 6 December 2008, http://www.ft.com/cms/s/0/33548be2-c33a-11dd-a5ae-000077b07658.html (last accessed December 2008)

107   OCHA (2008) *The Humanitarian Monitor,* Number 29, September 2008, www.ochaopt.org/?module=displaysection&section_id=118&static=0&edition_id=&format=html (last accessed November 2008).

108   UN OCHA Financial Tracking Service, *op.cit.*

109   Interview with Jane Beesley, Oxfam GB, January 2004.

110   The Sphere Project (2004) *Sphere Handbook: Humanitarian Charter and Minimum Standards in Disaster Response*, Oxford: Oxfam International.

111   Example taken from author's own experience.

112 See also J. Darcy and C.A. Hoffmann (2003) 'According to Need?', Humanitarian Policy Group Report 15, London: Overseas Development Institute, p. 5.

113 IASC (2006) *Women, Girls, Boys and Men: Different Needs – Equal Opportunities*, New York: IASC, p. 3.

114 T. Schümer (2007) *New Humanitarianism: Britain and Sierra Leone 1997–2003*, London: Palgrave.

115 A. Stoddard, A. Harmer, K. Haver, D. Salomons, and V. Wheeler (2007) 'Cluster Approach Evaluation: Final Draft', Geneva: IASC, p. 5.

116 C. Adinolfi, D.S. Bassiouni, H. Lauritzsen, and H.R. Williams (2005) *Humanitarian Response Review*, New York: United Nations.

117 *Ibid.*

118 *Ibid.*

119 In 1994, the Chair of the UN Inter-agency Standing Committee highlighted the need to '… [establish] a pool of candidates with the appropriate profile who were ready to serve as Humanitarian Coordinator at short notice, and for a clearly defined period' (Eighth Session of the IASC, 27 June 1994). For more information see www.icva.ch/doc00001438.html (last accessed November 2008).

120 G. Thomas (2008) 'Humanitarian Reform, Speech by Gareth Thomas, UK Minister of State for Development', www.dfid.gov.uk/news/files/Speeches/gareth-humanitarian-reform.asp (last accessed November 2008).

121 See the Humanitarian Reform website, www.humanitarianreform.org (last accessed November 2008).

122 S. Graves, V. Wheeler, and E. Martin (2007) 'Lost in Translation: Managing Coordination and Leadership Reform in the Humanitarian System', Humanitarian Policy Group Briefing Note No. 27, London: Overseas Development Institute, p. 2.

123 A. Donini, L. Fast, G. Hansen, S. Harris, L. Minear, T. Mowjee, and A. Wilder (2008) 'The State of the Humanitarian Enterprise', final report of Humanitarian Agenda: 2015, p. 13.

124 Interview with Jane Beesley, Oxfam GB, March 2008.

125 *Ibid.*

126 Humanitarian Policy Group (2008) 'Humanitarian Action in Iraq: Putting the Pieces Together', Humanitarian Policy Group Policy Brief No. 30, London: Overseas Development Institute.

127 Humanitarian Policy Group (2006) 'Providing Aid in Insecure Environments: Trends in Policy and Operations', HPG Briefing Paper No.24, London: Overseas Development Institute, p. 3.

128 H. Slim (2007) *Killing Civilians: Method, Madness and Morality in War*, Colombia: Hurst C & Co.

129 Humanitarian Policy Group (2008) *op.cit.*

130 G. Hansen (2007) 'Coming to Terms with the Humanitarian Imperative in Iraq, Humanitarian Agenda 2015', Briefing Paper, Feinstein International Center, Tufts University, p. 9.

131 UN Department of Safety and Security.

132 For example 'Oslo Guidelines on The Use of Foreign Military and Civil Defence Assets In Disaster Relief', http://ochaonline.un.org/AboutOCHA/Organigramme/ EmergencyServicesBranchESB/CivilMilitaryCoordinationSection/PolicyGuidanceandPu blications/tabid/1403/language/en-US/Default.aspx (last accessed November 2008).

133 Development Assistance Committee (1998) 'Civilians and Military Means of Providing and Supporting Humanitarian Assistance During Conflict', DAC/OECD Conflict Series, Paris, www.oecd.org/dataoecd/17/3/1886558.pdf (last accessed November 2008).

134 For a detailed analysis of military humanitarianism and Oxfam's position, see Oxfam International (2007) 'OI Compendium Note on the Provision of Aid by Military Forces', Oxford: Oxfam International, www.oxfam.org.uk/resources/policy/conflict_disasters/ downloads/oi_hum_policy_aid_military.pdf (last accessed February 2008).

135 North Kivu Protection Cluster (2007) 'Urgent Need to Protect the Population in North Kivu, in the Context of Renewed Conflict and Diminishing Coping Capacities', Goma: NKPC.

136 M. Anderson (1999) *Do No Harm: How Aid Can Support Peace – or War*, Boulder: Lynne Rienner; and T. Paffenholz and L. Reychler (2007) *Aid for Peace: A Guide to Planning and Evaluation for Conflict Zones*, Baden Baden: Nomos.

137 VOICE (2002) *Improving the Quality of Humanitarian Aid in Conflict Situations: Training for Good Practice*, Brussels: VOICE, p. 7.

138 L. Minear (2005) 'Lessons learned: the Darfur experience', in J. Mitchell, I. Christoplos, L. Minear, and P. Wiles, *ALNAP Review of Humanitarian Action in 2004*, London: Overseas Development Institute, pp. 111–12; and H. Young , A. Monim Osman, Y. Aklilu, R. Dale, and B. Badri (2005) 'Darfur 2005 Livelihoods Under Siege', Medford: Feinstien International Famine Center, Tufts University, p. 130.

139 Africa Peace Forum, Centre for Conflict Resolution, Consortium of Humanitarian Agencies, Forum for Early Warning and Early Response, Saferworld, and International Alert (2004) 'Chapter 5: Institutional Capacity Building for Conflict Sensitivity', in *Conflict-Sensitive Approaches to Development, Humanitarian Assistance and Peacebuilding: A Resource Pack*, London: Africa Peace Forum *et al.*, p. 2.

140 See also M. Lange (2004) *Building Institutional Capacity for Conflict-Sensitive Practice: The Case of International NGOs*, London: International Alert; and Africa Peace Forum *et al.* (2004), *op.cit.*

141 Focus-group discussion, women's group, Sithamparapuram camp (24 April 2002) in J. Boyden, T. Kaiser, and S. Springett (2002) 'The case study of Sri Lanka', for *ALNAP Global Study on Consultation and Participation of Disaster-affected Populations*, London: Overseas Development Institute.

142 Mango (no date) 'Top Tips on Reporting to Beneficiaries', www.mango.org.uk/guide (last accessed November 2008).

143 UNHCR (2002) 'Sexual Violence and Exploitation: The Experience of Refugee Children in Guinea', Geneva: UNHCR.

144 Oxfam (2006) 'Lessons Learnt in Preventing Sexual Exploitation and Abuse in Programme Delivery', internal background document, August.

145 *Ibid.*

146 SARPN, Concern, and Oxfam (2008) 'Strengthening responses to the triple threat in the Southern Africa region – learning from field programmes in Malawi, Mozambique and Zambia', www.reliefweb.int/rw/rwb.nsf/db900SID/KHII-6RP9WD?OpenDocument (last accessed November 2008), p. 4.

147 Oxfam (2003) 'Northern Uganda Humanitarian Strategy 2003–5', Kampala: Oxfam GB, unpublished. See also S. Addison (2008) 'Humanitarian space in a fragile state', *Forced Migration Review* 30: 69.

148 Interview with Jane Beesley, Oxfam GB, April 2007.

149 *Ibid.*

150 UNHCR (2005) 'Ogata calls for stronger political will to solve refugee crises', 27 May, www.unhcr.org/cgi-bin/texis/vtx/print?tbl=NEWS&id=4297406a2 (last accessed November 2008).

151 Figures from IFPRI cited on Reuter's AlertNet website, http://lite.alertnet.org/printable.htm?URL=/db/crisisprofiles/AF_HUN.htm&v=at_a_glance (last accessed November 2008).

152 UNICEF (2006) *Progress for Children: A Report Card on Nutrition, No.4,* New York: UNICEF, p. 6.

153 World Food Program (2008) 'How WFP Fights Hunger', www.wfp.org/aboutwfp/introduction/hunger_fight.asp?section=1&sub_section=1 (last accessed November 2008).

154 G. Ellerts (2006) 'Niger 2005: not a famine, but something much worse', *Humanitarian Exchange Magazine* 33.

155 Food donations have made up the largest share of commitments to CAP appeals, accounting for $12.2bn (54 per cent) of the $22.6bn committed to CAP appeals since 2000. Food is not only by far the largest sector; it is also the sector that is best funded in relation to requests. Development Initiatives (2008) 'Global Humanitarian Assistance 2007/2008', Wells: Development Initiatives.

156 See Oxfam International (2005) 'Food Aid or Hidden Dumping?', Oxfam Briefing Paper 71, Oxford: Oxfam International.

157 'Purchase for Progress', a proposal by WFP to the Gates Foundation, 2008.

158 See 'Billions "wasted" by aid system', BBC News, 18 September 2008, http://news.bbc.co.uk/1/hi/world/7622275.stm (last accessed November 2008).

159 Oxfam International (2008) 'The Time is Now: How World Leaders Should Respond to the Food Price Crisis', Oxfam International Briefing Note, Oxford: Oxfam International.

160 R. Slater, S. Ashley, M. Tefera, M. Buta, and D. Esubalew (2006) 'PSNP Policy, Programme and Institutional Linkages', ODI/IDL Group/Indak.

161 The Hyogo Framework for Action sets out three key strategic disaster risk-reduction goals: (1) The integration of disaster risk-reduction into sustainable development policies and planning; (2) Development and strengthening of institutions, mechanisms, and capacities to build resilience to hazards; and (3) The systematic incorporation of risk-reduction approaches into the implementation of emergency preparedness, response, and recovery programmes. See www.unisdr.org/wcdr/intergover/official-doc/L-docs/Hyogo-framework-for-action-english.pdf (last accessed November 2008).

162 For background on the scale of the emergency, see ECHO (2007) 'Emergency Humanitarian Aid in Favour of the Population of Bolivia Affected by the El Niño Phenomenon', Emergency Humanitarian Aid Decision, 15 March, www.reliefweb.int/rw/rwb.nsf/db900sid/DHRV-6ZW9VZ?OpenDocument (last accessed November 2008).

163 For more information on this project, see www.oxfam.org.uk/oxfam_in_action/impact/success_stories/bolivia_farming.html (last accessed November 2008).

164 Interview with Ravindranath, Director of Rural Volunteers Centre in Assam, 12 February 2007, Kolkata, in Oxfam International (2008) 'Rethinking Disasters', *op.cit.*, p. 20.

165 Development Initiatives (2008) *op.cit.*

166 See PricewaterhouseCoopers (2007) *op. cit.*

167 Stockholm International Peace Research Institute (2008) *SIPRI Yearbook 2008,* Oxford: Oxford University Press.

168 Development Initiatives (2008) *op.cit.*, p. 2.

169 N. Bennett (2008) 'No Way Home', 14 April, http://kristof.blogs.nytimes.com/author/nbennett (last accessed November 2008).

170 Ranked by 'per citizen' spend on humanitarian aid, they are: Luxembourg, Norway, Sweden, Denmark, Netherlands, Ireland, Switzerland, Finland, the UK, and Belgium.

171 Development Initiatives (2008) *op. cit.*

172 *Ibid.*, p. 14.

173 See OECD/DAC (2008) 'Survey of Aid Allocation Policies and Indicative Forward Spending Plans', www.oecd.org/dac/scalingup (last accessed November 2008).

174 K. Haver (2007) 'Diversity in Donorship: Field Lessons', Humanitarian Policy Group, London: Overseas Development Institute.

175 L. Cotterrell and A. Harmer (2005) 'Diversity in Donorship: the Changing Landscape of Humanitarian Aid', Humanitarian Policy Group, London: Overseas Development Institute.

176 Turkey and South Korea are members of the OECD but not of DAC.

177 Figures from UN OCHA's Financial Tracking Service (FTS), *op.cit.*

178 E. El-Hokayem (2008) 'The Arab Gulf States: Wealth in the Service of Humanitarianism and Status', unpublished paper for Oxfam America.

179 UN OCHA's Financial Tracking Service (FTS), *op.cit.*

180 Oxfam International (2008) 'After the Cyclone: Lessons from a Disaster', Oxfam International Briefing Note, Oxford: Oxfam International.

181 Figures derived from UN OCHA's Financial Tracking Service (FTS), *op.cit.* and UN Consolidated Appeal documents, www.humanitarianappeal.net (last accessed November 2008).

182 UN OCHA's Financial Tracking Service (FTS), *op.cit.*

183 B. Willits-King, T. Mowjee, and J. Barham (2007) 'Evaluation of Common/Pooled Humanitarian Funds in DRC and Sudan', report for OCHA ESS, http://ochaonline.un.org/OchaLinkClick.aspx?link=ocha&docId=1088368 (last accessed November 2008), p. 3.

184 N. Bennett (2007) 'Impact of Humanitarian Reform Mechanisms in the Democratic Republic of Congo (DRC)', unpublished paper written on behalf of Oxfam GB, www.humanitarianreform.org/humanitarianreform/Portals/1/H%20Coordinators/HC%20retreat/Day%201/OXFAM%20DRC%20discussion%20paper.doc (last accessed November 2008).

185 *Ibid.*, p. 3.

186 B. Willits-King *et al.* (2007) *op.cit.*

187 Oxfam International (2007) 'The UN Central Emergency Response Fund One Year On', Oxfam Briefing Paper 100, Oxford: Oxfam International, pp. 2–4.

188 N. Bennett (2007) *op.cit.*, p. 8.

189 J. Macrae, S. Collinson, M. Buchanan-Smith, N. Reindorp, A. Schmidt, T. Mowjee, and A. Harmer (2002) 'Uncertain Power: The Changing Role of Official Donors in Humanitarian Action', Humanitarian Policy Group Report 12, London: Overseas Development Institute.

190 'Principles and Good Practice of Humanitarian Donorship', endorsed in Stockholm, 17 June 2003, by Australia, Belgium, Canada, the European Commission, Denmark, Finland, France, Germany, Ireland, Japan, Luxembourg, Netherlands, Norway, Sweden, Switzerland, the UK, and the USA, www.goodhumanitariandonorship.org (last accessed November 2008).

191 S. Graves and V. Wheeler (2006) 'Good Humanitarian Donorship: Overcoming Obstacles to Improved Collective Performance', Humanitarian Policy Group Discussion Paper, London: Overseas Development Institute, p. 3.

192 S. Hidalgo and A. Lopez-Claros (2008) *The Humanitarian Response Index 2007*, London: Palgrave.

193 S. Graves and V. Wheeler (2006) *op.cit.*, pp. 12–14.

194 For more information visit MERCY Malaysia's website, www.mercy.org.my (last accessed November 2008).

195 *Zakat* is an obligatory annual donation of money made by all devout Muslims (equal to one-fortieth of one's assets other than home and resources necessary to work).

196 J. Benthall (2008) 'The Palestinian Zakat Committees', unpublished paper for Oxfam America.

197 See www.humanitarianforum.org (last accessed November 2008).

198 L. Altinger and V. Tortella (2007) 'The Private Financing of Humanitarian Action, 1995–2005', Humanitarian Policy Group Briefing Paper, London: Overseas Development Institute, www.odi.org.uk/hpg/papers/hpgbgpaper_monitoringtrends2.pdf (last accessed November 2008).

199 See TNT (2008) 'What's in it for TNT?', www.movingtheworld.org/what039s_it_tnt (last accessed November 2008).

200 A. Binder and J. Martin Witte (2007) 'Business Engagement in Humanitarian Relief: Key Trends and Policy Implications', Humanitarian Policy Group Background Paper, London: Overseas Development Institute, www.odi.org.uk/hpg/papers/hpgbgpaper_monitoringtrends1.pdf (last accessed November 2008).

201 See for example R. Kent and J. Ratcliffe (2008) 'Responding to Catastrophes: U.S. Innovation in a Vulnerable World', Washington, DC: Centre for Strategic and International Studies, p. 21.

202 For a more detailed analysis of the corporate sector as a humanitarian actor, see Oxfam International (2007) 'OI Policy Compendium Note on the Private Sector and Humanitarian Relief', Oxford: Oxfam International, www.oxfam.org.uk/resources/policy/conflict_disasters/downloads/oi_hum_policy_private_sector.pdf (last accessed November 2008).

203 Interview with Marie Cacace, Oxfam GB, August 2008.

204 These include the Geneva Conventions, the UN Human Rights Conventions, the UN Refugee Convention, the Red Cross Code of Conduct, OCHA Guiding Principles on Internal Displacement, and the IASC Operational Guidelines on Human Rights and Natural Disasters.

205 Oxfam International (2008) 'For a Safer Tomorrow', op.cit.

206 The Comprehensive Africa Agricultural Development Programme (CAADP) of the New Partnership for Africa's Development (NEPAD) is a an African Union-led, African-conceived process, designed to address issues of growth in the agricultural sector. See www.nepad.org/2005/files/home.php (last accessed November 2008).

207 Oxfam International (2008) 'Climate Wrongs and Human Rights', op.cit.

208 Oxfam International (2008) 'Rethinking Disasters', op.cit.

Index

Page numbers in *italics* followed by f or b refer to figures and boxes respectively